TRUE LOVE
TAROT

THE LOVER'S GUIDE
TO DATING,
MATING, AND RELATING

AMY ZERNER AND MONTE FARBER

THOMAS DUNNE BOOKS

ST. MARTIN'S PRESS ❧ NEW YORK

TRUE LOVE TAROT

For information, address St. Martin's Press, 175 Fifth Avenue, New York, NY 10010.
Library of Congress Cataloging-in-Publication Data available on request.

ISBN 0-312-33756-6
Thomas Dunne Books
An imprint of St. Martin's Press

First US Edition printed in 2006
10 9 8 7 6 5 4 3 2 1

Published simultaneously in Canada by St Martin's Press

Produced by Zerner/Farber Editions
Box 2299
East Hampton, New York 11937
www.TheEnchantedWorld.com

Designed by Elizabeth Elsas
Printed in China through Colorcraft Ltd., Hong Kong

WE DEDICATE

TRUE LOVE TAROT TO EACH OTHER

AND TO THE BLESSING OF

THE 30-YEAR RELATIONSHIP WE HAVE SHARED.

WE LOVE EACH OTHER MORE EACH DAY

AND PRAY TO TRAVEL INTO FOREVER,

TOGETHER.

THE MAJOR ARCANA

~

THE COURT CARDS AND THE MINOR ARCANA

~

THE SUIT OF ROSES

also known as Fire, Action, Batons, Wands, or Clubs

~

THE SUIT OF WINGS

also known as Air, Ideas, Swords or Spades

~

THE SUIT OF SHELLS

also known as Water, Emotions, Cups, or Hearts

~

THE SUIT OF GEMS

also known as Earth, Resources, Coins, or Diamonds

~

SPELLS FOR TRUE LOVE

~

INTRODUCTION

The tarot is the ultimate reality game because all of life
is contained in the cards of a tarot deck.

RUE LOVE TAROT is a unique map and guidebook that can enable soul mates to find each other and lovers to overcome obstacles, even today when the world can sometimes appear to be as dark as a cloudy night. It will provide you with the means for getting in touch with the quiet voice within you that knows, without a doubt, what is best for your greatest good and highest joy. Whether you want to improve your existing relationship or want to meet your soul mate, *True Love Tarot* can light your way.

In these exciting though challenging and turbulent times, people are seeking true love, comfort, and reassurance in their relationships and those without a partner are seeking one with urgency greater than usual.

When you look at today's high divorce rate and the growing number of people who choose to raise their children in single-parent households, you see the often harsh consequences of people outgrowing their partnerships and deciding not to settle for less than the loving relationship they feel they deserve. There is an art to bringing love into our lives. There are specific steps we can take to do so. We have created *True Love Tarot* to acquaint you with the art of love and to show you the steps that will help you to find the true love you seek.

We have distilled the powerful essence of all we have learned into this system so you can use it easily and enjoyably in the midst of your hectic day. It is our most sincere desire that the time you spend using our creation will entertain and empower you and help you find your way on the road to happiness and true love that lovers throughout time have tread.

KNOW THYSELF

~

For thousands of years, seekers wishing to act in harmony with divine forces have consulted the oracles of the various gods and goddesses. The most famous was the Temple of the Oracle at Delphi, a Greek island to which pilgrims made their way for many centuries to seek the wise counsel of the supreme oracle of the sun god, Apollo. It was there that the expression, "Know thyself," was found inscribed upon one of the two great pillars flanking the temple's entrance. On the other was the equally wise but lesser known admonition, "Nothing in excess."

The dictionary defines an oracle as:

   1. The answer *given since ancient times at a shrine as the response of the god or goddess to an inquiry.*
   2. The medium *giving such responses.*
   3. The shrine *where these responses were given.*

Like a hologram, each piece of the universe contains all the information necessary to recreate the whole universe. Throughout this limitless expanse, everything is connected to everything else. The interconnection and interdependence of all things is a basic premise of ancient wisdom and is a principle proven mathematically by the new chaos theory created by Benoit Mandelbrot. An oracle uses both our intuition and logical mind to receive and decode the information and then allows us to avail ourselves of it using a language we can understand.

The tarot is an oracle and a form of do-it-yourself analysis—a way of unlocking secrets of the self and providing direction toward manifesting your goals. It is a support system you can rely upon as a friend that can give you helpful advice. It is also a great brainstorming tool to enhance your creative decision-making abilities. Reading cards makes users more aware of their everyday surroundings, hopes, fears, pasts, and presents. It is an aid to decision making that highlights forces and influences in users' lives that might otherwise go unnoticed. It offers insight and new ideas. The tarot facilitates your mindfulness by tuning you in to a deeper inner level of awareness. It is a "book of knowledge" that offers a way to journey into yourself and discover your spiritual center. The seventy-eight cards portray all cycles of the human experience. Using the tarot, a focusing mechanism, also helps you develop your psychic abilities and empowers you to make the best choices in your life.

Each time you do a tarot reading, it is very important to evaluate what you think and feel about the answer you have gotten then make your decisions based on the heightened awareness the tarot brings to your situation. The tarot does not dictate your actions or your behavior. Rather than telling you what to do, the cards put you in touch with how you feel about what is going on in your life. After a while, you will notice your intuition and your ability to make decisions, with and without the aid of tarot cards, will improve.

The tarot adds spice to your life, but you cannot live on spice alone. Your free will to make decisions is your main course. It is our sincere desire that *True Love Tarot* will help you better understand your inner voice and its ability to direct you. We hope you come to know the power that has helped us so you, too, can make your relationships all you want them to be. If you approach the tarot with a sense of ceremony, sincerity, and humility, then all may be revealed to you.

In our opinion, divination is nothing less than getting in touch with the divine within all things. The tarot allows us to access the ultimate connectedness in the universe when we harness our logical and intuitive faculties.

BRINGING TRUE LOVE INTO YOUR LIFE

~

Introducing you to *True Love Tarot* and all it represents is a great honor and a privilege for me as an author and especially as a man. It is the result of thirty years of research by my wife and soul mate Amy Zerner and me. Amy and I are the artist and author respectively of *The Enchanted Tarot* and *The Instant Tarot Reader*. Since 1990 we have introduced hundreds of thousands of people to the fascinating and useful experience of using tarot cards to gain insight into their lives and the world around them.

Amy has been my partner since 1974. Together, we have dedicated our lives to using our art to make the timeless truths of ancient knowledge systems and personal power accessible and useful to everyone here and now in our modern world. We have succeeded in "brushing off the dirt" of centuries of misunderstanding and superstition from the golden treasure contained in many of the occult (meaning hidden or obscured) and divinatory arts—especially the tarot.

We have devoted our lives to making practical and life-affirming disciplines such as astrology, the tarot, and alchemy easily accessible to all. We put everything we have learned about creating our own successful relationship into *True Love Tarot* in the hope we might help other people enjoy their lives as much as we enjoy ours.

Many people are saddened by their apparent failure to bring true love into their lives. Common reasons they give for this situation are:

1. The right people are just not out there to be found.
2. Those who we are attracted to will not commit themselves.
3. We are not attracted to those who are attracted to us (and vice versa).
4. We feel we do not deserve any better than what we have (due to low self-esteem).

We can solve problems like these only if we replace the habit of putting into the hands of others the power to make us feel fulfilled, with more positive habits and insights that increase self-esteem. Each of us must accept the responsibility for creating our own happiness. *True Love Tarot* can help you do so. If you want to bring love, harmony, and success into your life you must accept the fact that you simply cannot change another person, no matter how hard you try. You can, however, change yourself.

As all successful people have learned, knowing as much as you can about the conditions that manifest in your life is crucial to making good decisions. As the old saying goes, "Forewarned is forearmed." If your tarot reading indicates things look like they are going to go well for you, then you know to keep doing things the way you have been doing them. If things look like they are not going to go well then the tarot also can suggest ways to make things go better.

Since childhood I have truly believed that the purpose of life is to be happy. Like everyone else, though, I have sometimes found myself not feeling happy at all. On one of those days I asked Amy, "What do you think is the common denominator of all human-caused suffering?"

Without a moment's hesitation she replied, "Poor decision making." Our *True Love Tarot* is designed to help you make better decisions and, thereby, make your life less stressful and more enjoyable. One of the things that prevents us all from making better decisions is we ignore the voice of intuition as it tries to guide us to making the right decisions. How many times have you said, "I knew I should (or should not) have done that but I didn't listen to my gut feeling"?

Our gut feeling *is* our intuition and it is speaking to us all the time. There are many reasons we don't listen to it and the biggest one is fear—not only fear of being wrong and embarrassed but also fear of being right and having our life change in ways we can't always control or predict. That is the point—we *can* predict the future and especially our future. I do it all the time as a professional psychic adviser to corporations. I enjoy using my psychic powers and my thirty years as a tarot reader and astrologer to tell them what's going to happen. Invariably, I'll tell them about how the relevant people in a situation are feeling and how they're most likely to act and react. I've saved people literally millions of dollars in time and money. The way I developed my psychic abilities was by writing and using our three tarot creations: *The Enchanted Tarot, The Instant Tarot Reader,* and *the Zerner/Farber Tarot Deck*. I'm not promising that you will become a highly paid psychic counselor as a result of using our *True Love Tarot* daily, but I do believe it will increase your intuition and empower you to make better decisions—and you may become psychic too!

It's fun to use your intuition to guide you. It's not spooky and if you do it to help yourself and those you care about lead happy, healthy lives filled with love, light, and laughter, then that is in keeping with the highest precepts of all religions. Amy and I believe the most spiritual thing anyone can do is truly be with the people with whom we interact—listening to their stories with compassion and the desire for complete understanding, learning what we can, and offering advice in a gentle, nonjudgmental way, if asked. Just because we know a lot doesn't mean anyone wants to listen to it.

The same holds true for using our *True Love Tarot*. It is hard for most people to admit their mistakes. It is painful to admit even to ourselves that we could have and should have been able to foresee the outcome of our decisions and the actions we took based upon those decisions. Deep down inside, however, it is hard for most people to deny that usually it has been their own poor decisions that have led to their difficulties. We grow by learning from these lessons, but we can also grow by getting to know ourselves better and learning how to make better decisions. That is what *True Love Tarot* is designed to do.

Like the value of true love, the value of proper decision making is one of the few things upon which everyone can agree. The mystic would say we create our own reality and, therefore, what we decide to create will determine what we experience. The more traditionally religious person would say our decision whether or not to be aware of our eternal oneness with the divine will determine whether we will suffer life's trials and tribulations with healing and acceptance or pain and rage. The hard-nosed, practical businessperson would say our decision-making ability determines how much power to rule our life we will accumulate on our brief journey on earth—the more power we possess, the better time we will have.

Our problems today are caused largely by the psychological consequences of too many people being ignorant of the inseparable connection between our inner and outer universe. We have created a modern world of spectacular technology that is in the hands of people who are out of touch with their ability to enjoy the simple gift of their being. They are so concerned about the results they are looking forward to that they have lost the ability to live in and be aware of what they are doing in the present moment, the only time that really exists. They are unable to enjoy what they have, and even when they get what they have been seeking, they are unable to enjoy it.

If we were not being distracted constantly with the thousand and one challenges of daily life, we would be able to hear our inner voice, what some people call the voice of our conscience or of our higher self. The gentle ritual of consulting the *True Love Tarot* makes an oasis of time and space in the middle of our daily routine that, in turn, allows us to be reconnected with the wisdom of what we all know deep within us. The ability for us to contact and make practical use of our innate powers was the highest goal of all schools of ancient wisdom.

True Love Tarot works on a heart-and-soul level to provide clear and insightful answers to your questions about finding, maintaining, and improving a loving relationship. Amy's gorgeous fabric collage tapestry images on the cards are meant to mimic nature's ability to put us in a state of relaxed concentration and contemplation. The beauty of her art enchants our souls and revives our spirits, breathing new life into our hopes, dreams, and wishes for the future. Each card has a title and a keyword to help you tune into the meaning right away. Whether used as a lighthearted party game or in moments of quiet reflection, my interpretations of the cards in the *True Love Tarot* guidebook can reveal unconscious beliefs about love—both those that draw love to us as well as those that keep us from the real love that is our birthright. By putting these timeless secrets into practice, you will be able to bring true love into your life.

We would like to thank you for giving us the chance to share the precious gift of the tarot with you, a gift that has enabled us to make our life a work of art and our art a work of life.

THE ORIGIN OF THE TAROT

~

There is an old joke told about every kind of scholar: Put two of them in a room and you will get three opinions. Some say the tarot—which travelers from India brought to Europe—started out as pasteboard pictures of various gods and goddesses used to teach their divine properties to the illiterate. These travelers arrived when Egypt was all the rage and found it advantageous to be known as Gyptees, ancestors of present-day Gypsies.

That theory might account for many people believing the tarot originated in Egypt. There are those who claim the tarot came from tenth century China, however, and there are advocates for Hebraic, Islamic, or Indian origins as well. One thing seems certain: The earliest and most complete deck of tarot cards dates from the early fifteenth century and is said to have been made for the Duke of Milan.

Egypt advocates say it derives from the words *tar* and *ro*, meaning the Royal Road. Indian advocates like to remind everyone else that the word *taru* means cards in Hindu and that *tara* is the Aryan name for the Great Mother Goddess. Those voting for tarot being a product of the Hebrew culture point to the word *Torah*, their name for the first five books of the Bible. Remember, though, that one of the areas where the cards first appeared was Milan, in Northern Italy, where the *Taro* River flows. Hm...

There are many who believe the first decks were as likely to have been used as a card game as they were for divinatory guidance. There is probably more than a little truth in that. The French word *tares* is used to describe the small dot border on playing cards.

The tarot came a long way in the twentieth century. The wisdom of the cards was an irresistible target for great artists, once they no longer feared persecution and ridicule. The tarot attracted both famous artists such as surrealist Salvador Dali and those undeservedly not so well known such as Pamela Coleman Smith who, under the watchful eye of Arthur Edward Waite, created what we now know as the Rider-Waite deck, the most famous tarot deck of the twentieth century. The origin of the tarot and even its original purpose is a subject upon which even the most learned scholars cannot seem to agree.

THE MAJOR ARCANA
AND THE MINOR ARCANA

~

The tarot may very well have started out as two separate decks: a spiritually oriented deck used for religious instruction and divination and the deck used for gaming and gambling.

THE MAJOR ARCANA are the first twenty-two cards of the tarot, starting with the number zero, THE FOOL, and going up to number twenty-one, THE WORLD. These cards represent the arcane or secret spiritual principles of life. We all make the journey from being THE FOOL, innocent and poised on the threshold of a great cycle of growth and experience, and eventually arrive at THE WORLD, our graduation and the culmination of a major period of our lives. Between these two cards are the twenty other major stages of growth and learning. Once we have gone through them all, we are ready to start again on our soul's quest for experience and self-knowledge.

THE MINOR ARCANA are not as concerned with spiritual realities as they are with our everyday earthly reality as human beings. The Minor Arcana help us bring the spiritual wisdom of the Major Arcana down to earth so we can use it for our benefit on all levels.

The Minor Arcana are the origin of the modern playing card deck whose four suits—clubs, spades, hearts, and diamonds—are the descendents of the tarot's traditional four suits—wands, swords, cups, and pentacles. Each suit has four court cards comprised of a king, a queen, a princess, and a prince. These represent the people you are involved with or an aspect of your personality you are dealing with at the moment. In *True Love Tarot*, the four suits are roses, wings, shells, and gems, representing, respectively, the energies of fire, air, water, and earth.

ROSES (fire) represent activity, energy, ambition, and social settings and situations. They also represent flirting, sex, and passion in relationships.

WINGS (air) represent communication, ideas, and power, as far as these concerns affect your relationships. They can also bring conflict, stress, hurt feelings, and anxiety.

SHELLS (water) refer to your emotional happiness, desires, and attention to beauty. They can also indicate sadness or disappointment.

GEMS (earth) represent practicality, success, and the material things in life. They could indicate finances, work, values, and property, as far as these concerns affect your relationships.

HOW DOES IT WORK?

~

The nearest thing to an explanation of why the tarot works is an ancient theory held by many peoples throughout the world and rediscovered in the twentieth century by the legendary psychologist Dr. Carl Jung. His theory of synchronicity (from the Greek *syn* meaning together and *chronos* meaning time) proposed that events happening at the same moment had a relationship of significance. In other words, when you ask your question with sincerity and you intend to get an answer, you will get an answer, possibly in many ways. It depends on how good you are at deciphering the events around you at the moment you ask the question. A flock of birds, cloud formations, or the pattern the wind makes in the trees could hold the answer. The tarot is a sort of sacred machine devised to respond to your question and freeze your answer as a picture of it in time so you may decipher it.

Using *True Love Tarot* as a meditation tool helps you dialogue with your higher self. Consulting the cards creates a safe, spiritual haven where you connect to positive energy and positive emotions. It helps you discover what you really want in life and what you must do as your next step on the path. And you can use the cards whenever you need clarity on an issue or as an everyday meditation. When you read your message, you can reflect upon your attitudes, desires, and strategies for the best course of action. The process requires opening your mind and trusting your intuition to interpret the answers. An oracle is a tool that helps you tap into your psychic power. And it can unlock the secrets to your heart.

HOW TO DO A READING

Choose a quiet location where you feel secure in the knowledge you will not be disturbed. It is important that you are properly prepared to ask your question. If you are not, you will not be able to receive accurate guidance and properly interpret your answer.

Trust in your higher self and you will not be disappointed. Do your best not to dwell on what answer you will get. That will stop the flow of the process of obtaining your answer.

STEP 1

How to ask your question

~

Experienced tarot readers know well that the tarot can answer any sincere question. The quality of the answer depends upon the clarity of the question and the skill of the tarot reader and the person who has asked the question in interpreting the answer the cards reveal.

Ask for guidance, saying either out loud or silently, one of the following basic questions or inquiries:

1. Tell me what I need to know about *(my date, my relationship, my meeting...)*.
   OR
2. Give me a message about *(this relationship, this friend, my trip...)*.

Here are some other sample questions about love and relationships phrased in such a way as to obtain the clearest answer from *True Love Tarot:*

· *Tell me what I need to know to about my love life.*

· *Tell me what I need to know now about finding my soul mate.*

· *Tell me what I need to know now about what is really going on in my relationship with...*

· *Tell me what I need to know now to improve my relationship with...*

· *Tell me what I need to know now about whether or not to end my relationship with...*

· *Tell me what I need to know now about calling...for a date.*

· *Tell me what I need to know now about my attitude towards love and relationships.*

· *Tell me what I need to know now about how to bring more love into my life.*

   OR

· *Give me a message about this person I am dating.*

· *Give me a message about getting back together with my boyfriend.*

· *Give me a message about my trying to save this relationship.*

· *Give me a message about dating my co-worker.*

· *Give me a message about telling my spouse I want a divorce.*

· *Give me a message about asking my lover about getting married.*

· *Give me a message about what to keep in mind now for my highest good and greatest joy.*

STEP 2

Repeat your question to yourself as you shuffle your True Love Tarot *card deck and pick a card to answer the question you have selected.*

~

Take a deep, luxurious breath and let it out slowly. Calm yourself and put everything else out of your mind. Pick up the deck and start shuffling it. As you shuffle, ask your question, either to yourself or out loud. As you say your question, see the situation you are asking about in your mind's eye. It might help you to close your eyes to do this. As you shuffle and ask your question, see your situation as if you are watching the action in a movie, on TV, or on a computer screen. This technique, called visualization, is very powerful.

If you are asking about meeting your soul mate or going out with someone new or someone you have never met, see yourself and the form of that person but with a question mark hovering where his or her face should be. If you are asking about someone you already know, visualize yourself with him or her and see the person's face, but see the question mark hovering above his or her head.

Then stop shuffling when it feels right to do so. Relax. You are doing fine. If you don't know when to stop shuffling, try shuffling for as long as it takes to ask your question two times. Make sure you phrase your question as a request, either as "Tell me what I need to know about..." or "Give me a message about..." That way, when you look up your card in the book, the advice and answer will make sense.

Next, put the deck face down and spread out the cards. Once again, take a moment to take another deep breath, calm yourself, and visualize your situation as clearly as you can in your mind's eye as you pick ONE card. If you are not comfortable visualizing your situation then say your question aloud as you pick your card.

Some people just cut the deck and take the card that is revealed, letting the card indicate their answer. The advantage of doing it this way is that it is very easy to do while you are shuffling. You do not have to put the cards down or even look at them until you have cut the deck and can see your card.

Other people like to take the top card, whereas others prefer to use the bottom card. Some people like to spread out the shuffled deck on a level surface and see which card calls to them. As long as your intention is strong and your mind is concentrated on the ritual of obtaining your answer, you will get the perfect answer to your question. The only things that could prevent this would be if you were worried about the answer you were going to get or attached to a particular kind of answer or thinking about something else instead of concentrating on your question. If you are anxious or distracted, you will not get accurate information.

If your card is upright, read the answer in the book that is noted as UPRIGHT. If your card shows upside-down, please read the REVERSED answer to your question. When you look at the card you have chosen, you will also notice a key word on the bottom of the card. This key word is an important message. Let that word speak to you.

IMPORTANT: Please note that you can ask YES and NO questions of the *True Love Tarot*. Simply follow the instructions, shuffle while thinking of your question, and look up your answer. You will find it on the card page next to the words UPRIGHT or REVERSED.

We all would prefer to hear just great news every day, but sometimes we have to wait and deal with what life has brought us. It is important to remember we all have lived through a number of challenges we worried about and doubted we could endure. Yet, somehow, we did endure. In most cases, nothing is ever as good or as bad as you think it is going to be. So take heart and ask your question in that state of relaxed contemplation, knowing you can deal with whatever answer you get and the *True Love Tarot* will offer helpful guidance to handle any difficult situation.

STEP 3

Look up the meaning of the card you selected

~

There is an index in the front of the book to help you quickly find the page with the meaning and message of the card you have chosen. Simply turn to the card's page and read your answer. The large majority of the answers you receive will make it seem as though the cards picked from your *True Love Tarot* deck are speaking directly to your question.

There may be times when the answer you receive does not appear to specifically answer your question. These are the best times for developing your intuition, your ability to read the cards, and your ability to make decisions. Open your mind to communicate with your higher self, the source of your inner intuitive voice. It does so using symbols, the language of your dreams and your subconscious mind.

Your first impression upon seeing the image of the card you have picked can inspire in your imagination a further series of images connected to and directed by your higher self. You may experience a flash of intuition that can reveal the meaning hidden from you only a moment ago. Many people who have never studied the tarot are able to read the cards. They go only by the impressions they receive from looking at the images on the cards. Amy's fabric collage tapestries have added her unique artistic statement to the tarot's many interpretations. She has been uniquely successful in blending the essence of the fantasy, fine art, and spiritual wisdom of all the nations thought to have originated the tarot. There is a wealth of information for you to draw on in each image.

There is also a logical process you must use in interpreting your reading with the *True Love Tarot* deck. You must remember to read the meaning of the card you have selected in the context of the question you have asked. Once you have asked the first question about a situation and received information about the basic conditions involved, you can then follow up with questions regarding timing.

It is good to suggest a time limit on your answer for purposes of clarity such as: "Tell me what I need to know about my date (today, tomorrow, this week, etc.)," or "Give me a message about how my relationship with my partner will progress during the summer season."

DEVELOPING YOUR INTUITION
~

Intuition is like a muscle. It can become stronger from being properly exercised. The best way to exercise your intuition is to use it consciously. When you learn to use and, most importantly, to trust your intuition, it will keep on getting stronger and stronger. We call a person with an extraordinarily developed mind a genius, and we call a person with an extraordinarily developed intuition a psychic.

Both these special groups of people are fairly rare in our society, but their existence is a reminder of the power of our brain. Scientists seem to be fond of saying how small a percentage of our brain's real abilities and power we actually use. I would like to suggest that one of the reasons studies show this is because a large part of the brain we are not using is connected with the abilities associated with our intuition. Unless we believe we have these abilities, how can we use them? That is why for most people, intuition comes in flashes, i.e., hunches, gut feelings, premonitions, or in precognitive dreams when our rational mind's culturally supported tyranny is absent and our intuition is free to work for us.

When you are using *True Love Tarot*, you are taking an important and powerful step towards fully developing your intuition. As you continue to exercise it, you will learn to trust it more.

WHAT IF YOU DO NOT LIKE THE ANSWER YOU RECEIVE?

~

When this happens, it is important to look inside yourself and see why you are troubled by the answer you have received. Do you have the confidence in yourself to believe you can cope with a wide range of experiences? If not, then why not? The wonderful thing about the tarot is that if you get an unfavorable answer, you can ask the tarot for guidance on how to change things for the better. Using the tarot to get in touch with your feelings is one of its most important uses.

CAN YOU DO A TAROT READING FOR ANOTHER PERSON?

~

Doing tarot readings for your friends is very enjoyable. It is usually best, however, to do your readings by yourself when you are first learning. *True Love Tarot* is designed so that you will learn quickly. Once you do, start with a trusted friend, preferably one with an open mind. Eventually you may feel confident enough to read for anyone, anywhere, anytime. Until then read and remember the answer to the next section. You will soon feel confident enough to try reading for another person.

CAN YOU DO A TAROT READING FOR SOMEONE WHO IS NOT PRESENT?

~

Wait until you are comfortable with the *True Love Tarot* procedure before trying to ask a question for someone who is not with you at the time you are doing the reading. Remember that most people do not understand what the tarot really is—a decision-making tool—and do not have the rest of the information contained in the book. Make sure the person understands what the tarot really is before attempting a reading for him or her. It is too easy to mislead or frighten the uninitiated if you ignore this advice.

Tell the person the answers they receive are only indications of the way things must be. They must understand that their free will is more powerful than any tarot reading. There is no reading so good that it cannot be invalidated if someone fails to do what is right. Conversely, there is no tarot reading that is so bad that it, too, cannot be invalidated by changing course and doing what is right. The tarot is a very powerful tool, but it is not more powerful than the people asking the questions. We, alone, are responsible for our actions.

If you remember and can convey this to those you want to do a reading for, you can rest assured the readings you do will help guide others. You will then be able to have a lot of fun learning about your life and life in general.

It is a tremendous responsibility to do readings for other people. This is something Amy and I enjoy even more than reading for ourselves, which we do every day.

A GENTLE REMINDER

~

Remember, the answer you get is your answer to your question and no one else's. When and if you ever feel like using your *True Love Tarot* in the presence of others, you will be amazed at how often the same answer means something different to practically every other person reading it. Sometimes everybody but the person who asked the question will understand the answer that comes up. It will be obvious that the person asking the question is refusing to see what is plain to everyone else. Be as gentle with that person as you would want him or her to be with you. People are very vulnerable when they ask questions about love. Everyone you trust enough to participate in your *True Love Tarot* session should honor this vulnerability with patience and the faith that we all come to understand what we can when we can. To go faster than we are able to comprehend will benefit no one.

Finally, *True Love Tarot* obviously gives answers to your questions about love and relationships, but are we dealing with answers that are our fate? What about our free will?

If there is one thing I am sure of in this world, it is that our *free will is stronger than anything*. If you get an answer you do not like or agree with, one that denies what you feel with all your heart to be true, accept the challenge to alter your fate. I am not saying it is going to be easy. I am saying that it can be done.

Ask the *True Love Tarot* for advice on what you can do to triumph over the way things seem to be going for you and your love life. The cards will do their best to help you if you will do your best to put their advice into daily practice. Just getting an answer is not going to bring true love into your life. Taking the actions indicated by that answer will almost certainly help you do so.

THE
MAJOR ARCANA

0. THE FOOL
TRUST

UPRIGHT: Yes! Have fun!

You are blessed! THE FOOL card upright means all things are possible for you now. It is a time for prayers to come true. THE FOOL represents the absence of fear, so take heart because a new adventure is beginning! Even an existing relationship becomes renewed when THE FOOL appears.

THE FOOL's colorful garb symbolizes personal freedom, so be yourself and don't be afraid to be different. Have faith, another trait of THE FOOL, that you are entitled to enjoy the gift of your life and share it with someone else. It's time for fun with a remarkably positive person who loves life and has a great sense of humor—even if there is an age difference between you—and if you're funny, too, so much the better! Don't say no to an invitation that seems to be too frivolous or "young" for someone your age.

THE FOOL always tells the truth and indicates that you are hearing it from others. A great relationship can be yours if you can put your past behind you and be the self you were when you where a pure and innocent child. Forget the past. Experience the present moment to the full.

Appreciate everyone and everything for the miracle that life is. You can risk seeming a bit foolish, naïve, or overly optimistic. Trust in a higher force to guide and protect you and your relationship. Take a chance, have fun, and see what happens.

REVERSED: No, don't be foolish!

You don't have to be a people pleaser to find true love—be yourself! Don't act silly, gossip, or allow anyone to make a fool of you. Consult a trusted advisor to find out if the way you present yourself to others needs a makeover. The way others see you may be far different from what you'd like. You or your partner may actually be or only appear younger than you are, but either way it works against you.

You may be deluded about another person or fooling yourself about a problem in the relationship. You may be involved with or attracted to a person who is wrong for you. Your hopes about the future of your relationship might be unrealistic, and the other person might have a completely different picture.

You may yearn for freedom, adventure, or a new cycle in your love life to begin, but unless you deal with the important issues at hand, you'll just keep running into the same problems in different relationships. Fun and games are no substitute for making good decisions. There may be too little planning and even less of the hard work it takes to have a great relationship.

Be less impulsive and more discerning. Don't take things on faith. Trust your head, not your heart. You will never experience true love with a love interest who is too harsh, egotistical, judgmental, or who has no sense of humor.

UPRIGHT: Yes! There's magic in the air!

Miracles can happen! The image on THE MAGICIAN card shows him radiating power as he hangs the sun in the sky, playing a tune and singing along with a bird. THE MAGICIAN card upright means a powerful, magical partner is likely to come into your life now. This person may even be "the one." In an existing relationship, a way will be found to create some new and special magic in your life together.

Now is the time to make magic by working your will on the world, not passively waiting for things to happen. It is time for you to be supremely confident and willing to take a chance on love.

There will be a magic moment when you look into your lover's eyes and you are totally turned on to each other. You will create the kind of relationship where you both feel stimulated and interested in everything the other says and does.

You may need to personally manipulate things a bit to make your desires your reality by taking the first bold step. Have the courage to believe you are a magical soul. If you are alone, tap into the infinite energy of the universe with visualization—use this powerful method to manifest the relationship you seek. Take a few deep breaths and try to see what you want in your mind's eye. Take time each day to affirm your dreams, hopes, and wishes for true love.

REVERSED: No, don't push it.

There is reason for concern about whether there is magic in this relationship. If you're looking for a relationship there may be reluctance to commit or even to just show interest because of fear of rejection. A lot of doubt may arise as a result of past relationships not working out. Passivity, doubt, and a lack of self-confidence may also be stopping someone from taking the first step. Both people involved need more assurance from the other that their affections are mutual before the magic of trust can bring true love.

It may be hard for you to stand up for yourself or take the initiative to make a relationship happen with a person you're attracted to. You may have to face the fact that, try as you might, you cannot make things go the way you want. You may discover that you do not have the energy and resources to resolve your situation favorably right away. Or you may experience someone trying to control you to make things happen their way. This is an indication that though they try to appear powerful, they are weak and afraid of their weakness being discovered.

Work on your resolve to stay positive, even though you have experienced sadness or rejection. Try to welcome new opportunities as they come instead of retreating into an unhealthy self-image that will be off-putting to anyone you are involved with, not just lovers.

2. THE HIGH PRIESTESS
INTUITION

UPRIGHT: Yes! Your hunch is right.

The crown THE HIGH PRIESTESS wears symbolizes a woman with amazing abilities, so you are either going to be that person in your quest for love or else you can expect to meet her in some form. Either way, your love life and relationships are going to improve in miraculous ways that seem blessed by a higher power.

THE HIGH PRIESTESS invites us to realize and appreciate all of the everyday miracles we take for granted, especially the miracle of feminine wisdom and power. When she appears to you in answer to a question about your relationship it is a sign that you should listen to your intuition, unclouded by the desire for a particular outcome. The best way to improve the situation you've asked about is through the power of inspiration, prayer, and the knowledge that what you want is right and good for you and your partner, if you have one. Relax, stop trying so hard, and let love come to you.

Focus on the things that inspire you, the things that give you goose bumps, not the usual mundane things. These things can be as simple and lovely as a child's laughter or a favorite pet's antics or as deep and beyond words as how you feel about the nature of personal reality, religion, the universe, and your place in it. When you feel inspired you will be inspiring, one of the most attractive qualities possible.

REVERSED: No, you ignored your intuition.

THE HIGH PRIESTESS reversed balances precariously on her crown, separated from Earth, its practicality, and the use of logic. Intuition is a powerful tool but, like true love, it works only when you are forgiving, not angry; inspired, not intoxicated; and respectful of the unknown, not fearful. Becoming overly dependent on intuition alone and intuition-building tools like *True Love Tarot* is as bad as not using them as a part of your decision-making process. You give the cards their power, not the other way around. Or you or your partner may not respect intuition, religion, or things metaphysical like the tarot, astrology, and psychic phenomena.

In either case you and/or your partner need to examine your attitude towards women—especially women of power (including mystical or spiritual power). Don't allow your partner to disrespect and/or control you because "women are not (or are) supposed to do that." And be especially careful that you have not allowed that kind of thinking to poison your own mind and prevent THE HIGH PRIESTESS within you from giving your life spiritual power.

Conversely, you may be undervaluing the role of men and the masculine principle. There are lots of good men who are trying to better themselves and gain the true power that comes when we control our impulses. The men and women we enter into relationships with are a reflection of how comfortable we are with the masculine and feminine sides of our personalities.

UPRIGHT: Yes! It's a beautiful thing!

THE EMPRESS walks in her wondrous garden with her beloved daughter following in her footsteps, learning the ways of the court and the most benevolent way to rule the nations under their family's authority. Upright, this card represents fertility, political connections, and material wealth that comes from the riches of the land, water, and sky. THE EMPRESS indicates a person who is attractive and very creative. Rejoice! Your love life is going to improve in ways that seem to show the guiding hand of a master artist.

In your quest for love, you can expect either to meet or be a person who exemplifies some or all of these qualities or those described below. If it is you that is to emulate THE EMPRESS, then you need to give birth to something that has never been. THE EMPRESS symbolizes Mother Nature giving birth to the natural world of love, peace, and beauty. If your question was about having a child, the answer is a very fortunate one. To make certain, pick a second card. If it is the Princess of Shells, the answer is almost certainly yes.

Making art or inventing something is similar to giving birth, so you may meet an artist or innovator. Your love life and relationships would benefit from your beautifying your appearance and/or that of your home, inside and out, in ways that you might ordinarily consider too expensive or luxurious. Buy flowers for yourself and expect to receive a beautiful bouquet or gift.

REVERSED: Maybe, if you get creative.

THE EMPRESS reversed shows her luxurious robes preventing her from using her hands to right herself and help her daughter. This symbolizes that your love life and relationships may suffer because of an overemphasis on the importance of outward appearances, wealth, and status.

Efforts to create a healthy and whole relationship may not be recognized and/or bear fruit in ways you hope. A nurturing, creative, and talented person may get his or her feelings hurt because of a sensitive nature. You are counting on help from someone but they may have another agenda.

This card reversed could indicate a withholding of love, possibly due to mother issues. Or being a mother might be all-consuming at the moment, leaving little time for romantic ventures.

If you desire to give birth to a new child or a creative project, wait until you have enough time and resources to do it without skimping. Or, there may be problems caused by your attitude towards having children or past incidents regarding fertility. In rare cases, this card could indicate problems caused by your child and/or the child of a partner—problems that restrict the relationship, your wellbeing, and/or resources.

The most likely manifestations of THE EMPRESS reversed are that circumstances may prevent you from improving your appearance—hold off on that shopping spree!—or fixing up your home, or you may be frustrated when you are unable to implement all of your creative ideas to find and keep true love.

4. THE EMPEROR
POWER

UPRIGHT: Yes!

THE EMPEROR shows his son a former battlefield where he defeated the four kings who are now his loyal representatives. They both carry half a shield, a symbol of the desire for peace that marks all great rulers, but they hold weapons, too, just in case.

Have no doubt that you will make true love appear in your life—THE EMPEROR commands it and he is the boss of bosses! In your quest for love expect either to meet or be a person who exemplifies some or all of the qualities of THE EMPEROR: authority, strength, aggressive for noble purpose, proud, and confident from genuine accomplishment. It will accompany a big improvement in your status and maybe even your wealth.

A relationship opportunity might present itself with an authority figure of some kind, maybe at work with someone in management or someone who is influential in your career. It might also involve an older person, perhaps even a sort of student/teacher situation. In any case, a team may be formed that has the potential to be powerful, motivated, and successful.

If you are in a relationship, you and/or your partner will respect each other's power and be able to put together the resources and connections to accomplish great things for your relationship. Be aware that displays of strength may create strong physical attractions and/or vibrant, sexy encounters. If so, then you must call the shots and don't take no for an answer.

REVERSED: No.

THE EMPEROR card reversed reveals that he and his son seem to have impossibly flat feet. This symbolizes that by toeing the line—the way authority must to maintain power—they have lost some of their humanity.

You and/or your partner are demanding to be recognized as a strong, imposing figure of unquestioned achievement or authority but it is working against you. If you are attracted to or already involved with a partner who is domineering or very opinionated, don't give up too much of your own power. True love requires neither party always be the one in charge.

Either you or someone you like may be emotionally distant or running away from intimacy and commitment. If you are needy for approval, it may be because you didn't get enough approval or affection from a parent or some other authority figure. This might cause you to be attracted to older people of wealth, power, and accomplishment, but be careful that they do not use their experience to take advantage of you. You may be tempted to sublimate your quest for true love to your quest for career advancement, wealth, and status.

THE EMPEROR reversed warns you to focus your attention completely on your goal now or you miss an opportunity. Do not delude yourself. If you try to be too logical, you will have difficulty expressing your feelings. Become aware of your deep desires or emotions, but do not reveal your secret plans, feelings, or weaknesses.

5. THE HIEROPHANT
TRADITION

UPRIGHT: Maybe, if you go by the book.

THE HIEROPHANT is an interpreter of arcane knowledge and sacred mysteries from humanity's earliest times. In this card we see the powerful shaman contemplating a stone sculpture of a wise being from his tribe's distant past before using its secret spell to awaken his sleeping lover.

You encounter or have to become a wise teacher. A spiritual practice like meditation, affirmation, or tarot can guide you on the path to true love. That path could be a wedding aisle, for THE HIEROPHANT blesses unions in formal matrimony and reunites lost loves, too, but only if you go by the book.

If you are looking for love, present yourself as a representative of the best your culture has to offer. You can best stand out by fitting in—using established styles, manners, and methods so well that you impress and attract a wonderful lover. Don't try to impress potential partners with how wild and unpredictable you are and don't get involved with any type of nonconformist, either.

If you are in a relationship, you must calm down, take the high road, and be the wise, serene teacher. Being conservative and traditional matters now. You must draw clearly defined boundaries and roles.

In any case, make sensible decisions. Avoid drugs, alcohol, and even the hint of sexual promiscuity. Play it safe, act like an adult, and stay on your best behavior. If you do, your friends and family will love you and your partner.

REVERSED: No.

THE HIEROPHANT reversed seems curled up in the fetal position symbolizing a return to childish insecurity and unacceptable acting out that comes when established rules, social mores, and other tools that distinguish adult, civilized behavior are forgotten or ignored.

Grow up! If you are looking for love, childish fantasies may be working against you. Or you may be presenting yourself as too old, too conservative, or too traditional to attract the kind of person you seek. Going by the book all the time can be overly restrictive and boring. Reuniting with someone from your past is not in the cards.

The differences between you and another may be irreconcilable. Whether one of you is trying to force the other to go by his or her rules or to rebel against long established traditions, the controlling person will become very unpopular, especially with respected family members.

No one should ever get so stuck on having to be right that he or she refuses to be open to other ways of thinking or believing. Inflexibility, especially about religion or politics, will produce arguments that make relationships unhealthy. Rules, regulations, and laws can also cause problems in your relationships now. Be careful about a big move or other big changes in lifestyle or ethics. Beware of unusual behavior—including spiritual practices—that create stress on your relationships. You cannot offer or be offered the advice, comfort, or support your love life needs right now, except by your *True Love Tarot*, of course!

6. THE LOVERS
ATTRACTION

UPRIGHT: Maybe, choose wisely.

THE LOVERS shows a landed nobleman kissing a simple girl who works for him. Will he chose love or the expectations of his station in life? Will she give herself to him fully or run away from a love that cannot be?

Is the love you seek a dream or is it reality? Someone will soon make you feel complete, someone you feel is worthy of your devotion and companionship, and there will seem to be love, affection, romance, and a satisfying relationship to experience.

Get in touch with what is truly attractive to you. You need to choose wisely between two or more equally attractive allurements. You must choose between what you have and what you think you want and may actually have. You may have to choose between two people or between love and lust or between two possible partners.

Know that someone else is feeling the same way you are—in love! If you are questioning whether to get involved with a particular person, then go for it. Your advances will be reciprocated. You may be thinking of marriage and commitment, but this card is about love affairs and romance—don't get ahead of yourself! THE LOVERS card shows that the energy of a sincere and lasting relationship is right around you. Be a brave, true lover and follow your bliss, for THE LOVERS upright means you will choose or have chosen wisely.

REVERSED: Maybe, choose wisely.

THE LOVERS reversed indicates you may choose or have already chosen unwisely regarding a choice between two or more people or equally attractive things or plans of action—between what you have and what you think you want. Know you can choose wisely only if you feel satisfied with who and what you are right now.

Poor decision making is the cause of most suffering. A painful decision must be made soon, possibly involving an illicit love affair. It may be hard to resist temptation and someone's feelings could get hurt. Someone may not make the choice you are seeking. True love may be blocked by self-gratification, adolescent infatuations, or looking at someone as an object or possession.

Be aware that you may be fantasizing. Insecurity, jealousy, doubt, and criticism may be the result of fear, especially fear of commitment. Or you may feel some kind of imbalance such as your love is more genuine than your lover's and/or that your relationship is no longer moving forward towards a common goal. One of you may be demanding more than the other is willing or able to give.

You may be so afraid of making the wrong choice that you wait too long and/or drive away someone who truly cares for you. Mixed feelings abound, as past experience has made it difficult for you to believe a true-love relationship could actually be experienced by anyone, especially you.

7. THE CHARIOT
DETERMINATION

UPRIGHT: Yes, go for it!

THE CHARIOT's heroic figure astride Pegasus symbolizes that it's time to marshal all the forces available to you to make true love real in your life, even if you have to fly to do it. You need to focus completely on your love life and relationships now because big improvements are possible in ways you can see and cannot see.

Don't allow yourself to be distracted or sidetracked—get in the race and win it. Don't think a better time than now is going to come along soon. Procrastinate and you will lose.

You must be the driver now of the situation or of an actual vehicle or other means of transportation. If some kind of a travel is involved in the situation and you can't drive a car, ride a bicycle, ski, snowboard, roller skate, skateboard, etc., then take lessons and learn or make the trip some other way. This is not the time to stand still. Make your move and do it now!

You need to be strong to withstand the rigors of what is required, so work out and exercise to the best of your ability. Give your body what it needs to be all that it is capable of being. If you are as fit as you can be, striving towards your goal will be almost as satisfying as attaining it. By harnessing your willpower, self-control, and self-confidence, you will win.

REVERSED: No, don't try so hard.

You may be in a race you can't win or focusing so single-mindedly on attaining true love that you are overlooking an important fact and losing your way. Poor planning and preparation may produce action or inaction that causes confusion, misunderstandings, and hurt. Lack of resources and/or insensitivity to your situation will block the results you desire.

Resentment will threaten even the best relationship. Don't let anyone take you for a ride. Being timid will make a love interest feel uneasy. If you are overly polite or too shy, build a bridge and get over it! Speak your mind and your heart, or true love will pass you by.

Distance, direction, and/or matters of transportation and travel may be insurmountable obstacles. Or you may be feeling that your love life is going nowhere.

The level of health or fitness by one or both of you may be causing problems. One of you may be unclear about how important the physical, emotional, or mental level of a relationship is to the other. You must compromise or suffer the consequences, even if you are exhausted.

Manipulation or competitiveness may be blocking you. True love is not about winning and losing. You could be confused by the motives or signals of the other person. You might be paralyzed with fear of doing something you will regret. Conversely, you will regret it if you and/or your partner move too quickly or come on too strong.

8. STRENGTH
UNDERSTANDING

UPRIGHT: Yes!

The lady and the tiger! When you embody STRENGTH upright you can have it all! The infinity sign hovering over the woman's head silhouetted against the emotional Moon, which is, itself, hidden by a hard man-made column and a tough mist-shrouded tree, symbolizes that your situation is blessed by infinite wisdom and you will have the strength and positive energy to establish a wonderful relationship soon. The key to creating a relationship of true love is that you have to be working on yourself to develop true strength—spiritually, mentally, emotionally, and physically. You have to balance the aspects of you that are human, animal, and divine. It may seem impossible but love, kindness, and a brave heart can bring them into balance. Only when you have developed these qualities in yourself can you recognize them in another person and be recognized by them in return.

You may soon know what heroism is by seeing someone you care about being courageous or by you, yourself, helping someone in need. Being a good lover means you are a good friend, too, sharing the ups and downs of life together with patient regard and concern for each other's wellbeing. Enduring difficult times together can make a relationship stronger.

If you are accepting of another's wounds and weaknesses, you can create a strong relationship built on fidelity and reassurance. Use compassion and understanding to express yourself, not force, anger, or brute strength.

REVERSED: No, it's too exhausting.

Animal instincts may get the better of spiritual intentions. The power of love may not triumph over force, coercion, and extremism. Faith may be challenged or weakened and the desired outcome may not be obtained. There may be a tendency to feed on the weaknesses of another—to dominate, control, and exploit vulnerabilities for personal benefit. Beware of encountering or displaying cowardice. Don't let fear stop you from doing what is right.

If someone is trampling on your self-expression or creativity then there is not a true-love bond between you. The truly strong derive their strength from the power of being true to themselves and from the power of true love, not from bending people to their will. Arrogant behavior can indicate that the partner's feelings are seen as unimportant. If you are caught in a power struggle, take steps to move in a more positive direction. You must protect yourself and your interests.

Don't give away your power because of loneliness or desperation. If you feel dependent on another because of material reasons or for protection, there may be resentment and a lack of true love. You cannot remain faithful to an empty relationship.

Do not play the role of victim, but do not tolerate any abuse or indignities. If there are children involved, they can suffer mightily from this dysfunctional behavior as well. Beware. People who feel weak and desperate abuse others and desperate people do desperate things!

9. THE HERMIT
INTROSPECTION

UPRIGHT: Yes, if you do it your way.

THE HERMIT is like a solitary, socially challenged, absent-minded professor, never in the picture but off to the side observing it. Whether moving toward society to offer wise guidance to a chosen few or away from it, THE HERMIT walks alone, more comfortable speaking with his bird friend than with most human beings—they usually let him down.

The best thing for your love life now is to be true to yourself and walk your own path. If you go out, spend time with people who understand you and like you just the way you are. If people who like and understand you aren't available, either go out by yourself or stay home alone or with a special someone or at least someone you know won't disappoint you. One unfailing sign of true love is if the two of you just like to be together anywhere and watch each other enjoy life.

THE HERMIT describes someone who is a loner, not a joiner. If it's you that is to be THE HERMIT, then you need to act mature or, ideally, display the true power of a master. It's hard to meet THE HERMIT. He or she can be an antisocial eccentric, but can also be a genius who is tired of not being understood by more average folk. If you come across someone with the good qualities of THE HERMIT, be yourself! THE HERMIT can spot a phony a mile away.

REVERSED: Maybe, but you need help.

You will not find true love unless you make more of an effort to accommodate the legitimate needs of other people. No matter how misunderstood you feel, don't act like it's a waste of your time or energy explaining or defending yourself to people not worthy to be in your presence. Acting superior or inferior will work against you now.

Don't do everything by yourself. Staying out of circulation or just feeling isolated will work against you and may lead you to act unwisely and become unpopular. By not reaching out to others, you cannot get the love and help you need.

THE HERMIT reversed means you are challenged in your efforts to walk any path you consider important. You may outsmart yourself without wise counsel. You may want to follow a particular teacher, take certain classes, or work on a project that requires total concentration, but it might be difficult for you to do so.

Age or eccentricity may become a problem. An older or eccentric person may let you down. Someone may develop a crush on a friend or counselor who has an entirely different view of the relationship. Foolish or immature actions could result.

You might be unable to read your situation accurately, so don't jump to conclusions—good or bad—about someone's behavior, ideas, or personality traits. Forgetfulness, coldness, or even harsh feelings may lie beneath the surface. Give yourself time alone to carefully consider your situation before you act.

10. THE WHEEL OF FORTUNE
LUCK

UPRIGHT: Maybe, take a chance.

THE WHEEL OF FORTUNE has spun and your lucky number has come up. Luck is preparation meeting opportunity and skill , so if you've prepared yourself for love and better relationships then you're that much better off. But even if you haven't, THE WHEEL OF FORTUNE indicates you're going to be quite lucky and in ways you never dreamed. You're now in an up cycle, so enjoy yourself while it lasts.

If you're looking for love, be positive and optimistic. Don't even think about the negatives. You may find love by visiting places where sports, gambling, and fun are celebrated. Any place that has a prominent circle as part of its name or architecture might also work for you such as a circus with its big top and Ferris wheel or even a cruise ship with its round portholes!

Your new partner could also be a gambler or "investor"—a more socially acceptable title for professional gambler—or otherwise involved with gaming, sports, or cycles, both the kind you study and the kind you ride. This indicates a broad range of activities, from those involved with marketing to those who build, maintain, or even race vehicles.

If you are in a relationship the good times are back! To jump-start your good fortune, take a vacation to a place that is known for one or more of the fun things described above. You may even want to try your luck as a contestant on a game show!

REVERSED: Maybe, but don't bet on it.

All bets are off, so don't take any unnecessary chances. If you have not prepared well or behaved honorably, this is a time of challenges. You may feel like you are on a downward spiral. If so, realize you are reaping what you have sown.

Progress in relationships might not be made as quickly as you would like. Your responsibilities might increase, making it difficult to take risks with your time and resources.

Circumstances seem to make it difficult to harmonize your plans with those of a love interest, new or old. Your reflexes and timing may be off and that can make you feel unlucky. Frustrations can harm relationships when schedules have to be changed, appointments are missed, and dates have to be cancelled.

Luck is the meeting of opportunity, preparation, and skill, so make sure you put effort into areas of life that you might be taking for granted. This card reversed can also mean it is time to give up on something that is not working out. Or it can indicate that a relationship has come full circle and you must be creative or lucky if the relationship is to survive. Don't get bogged down by old patterns that no longer serve you, or by being unreceptive to a new opportunity because it will take you in a new direction. Progress can be made only if you let go of unrealistic expectations. Remember, peace begins when expectations end.

11. JUSTICE
TRUTH

UPRIGHT: Yes, you deserve it.

THE ANGEL OF JUSTICE dispenses flowers from her overflowing basket, symbolizing that you will get what you deserve and more. Truth and beauty will prevail over ignorance and negativity. Legal matters or negotiations will be settled fairly. Making improvements in your home, your relationship, and your lifestyle is a realistic and attainable goal now.

If you are looking for love, prepare to meet a wonderful partner soon. He or she may be quite attractive and/or connected to the justice system in some way or involved with any kind of activity that makes the world more beautiful and just. He or she will definitely be nice and kind. JUSTICE is one of the cards that indicates a happy marriage is possible now!

Existing relationships will improve dramatically. A balance will be reached creating mutual understanding and acceptance. Speak the truth and be fair and just with all. You are correct in your ability to detect honesty or dishonesty in yourself and others. Both parties need to give and take, trusting the bond of true love. This is a good time to put things in writing such as a prenuptial agreement or marriage contract, or otherwise consult the legal or counseling system to make things clear and fair.

The JUSTICE card also symbolizes peace and all the good and sweet things in life that can be enjoyed during a time of peace—an improving environment, a loving family with time for each other, and a fair government of involved citizens.

REVERSED: No, it's just not right.

THE ANGEL OF JUSTICE crashes to Earth, symbolizing that—in this case—truth, beauty, and justice will not prevail over ignorance and negativity. This can also indicate a time of actual hostility or impending strife. You or the two of you have got to act like angels or there are going to be things said and done that may have lasting negative consequences.

In legal and other matters, you may not get what you deserve this time. Agreements may not be made or upheld. Judgments may seem unbalanced and unfair.

If you are looking for love, THE ANGEL OF JUSTICE reversed can mean that your preconceived requirements for a partner are unreasonable or will not be met. The truth may not be told by you or another. Void self-deception. Those close to you and/or to someone you're interested in may not be telling the truth. Avoid or postpone any kind of commitments that are asked of you.

JUSTICE reversed can indicate problems caused by you and/or your partner's faithfulness, truthfulness, appearance, and personal hygiene. Someone in the relationship believes there's inequality and one-sidedness that stifles true love. Both sides are certain they are right. A tit-for-tat attitude causes rigidity and mistrust. In disagreements, a stalemate will be the best you can hope for. Your emotional commitment to a relationship may not be reciprocated. Agreements regarding wealth, possessions, children, physical attributes, or marriage will challenge even the best efforts to create and maintain true love.

UPRIGHT: Maybe, if you change your perspective.

THE HANGED MAN is upside down but is he really hanging? His right hand is planted squarely on the ground to support him and the rope tied around his right foot is loose, not taut. Is he a weak soul punished for his transgressions about to be hoisted up and left to the elements? Or is he incredibly strong and doing a one-handed handstand to prove it with a safety rope wisely tied around his ankle to catch him if he falls?

THE HANGED MAN card upright symbolizes the two ways we can approach difficult times. When life as we know it seems turned upside down we have a choice—will we face facts and deal with a completely new set of challenges or will we let fear and inertia make us dizzy, paralyzing our will and actions?

Whether you're looking for love or have a relationship, you and any partner, real or imagined, have got to have a great attitude and be able to deal well with adversity—no weak people need apply. Both people have to be strong and open enough to be able to change their minds about the most fundamental things possible. Any relationship surviving this difficult time will probably last.

Take a time-out to find the higher meaning in your life. Do yoga, meditate, or use any method you believe can help you release stress and transcend your hang-ups. If you view your relationship from a new perspective, positive change will occur.

REVERSED: Maybe, if you don't panic.

THE HANGED MAN reversed seems to be in a state of panic, trying to run with his arms flailing wildly, ignoring the rope around his ankle that is going to trip him up if he doesn't watch out.

If you are looking for love, don't let your anxiety about ever finding it color your interactions with potential partners. You may drive yourself crazy and other people away from you if you obsess about this time of suspended animation and try to rush things. Don't panic or you'll trip yourself up.

Single or coupled, this is a time of difficulties that are beyond your control. You may feel unjustly punished (and you may be right!) and stuck in a relationship that is getting worse. What you thought was true love may have turned out to be co-dependency. A counselor or therapist may be required to help you both see things from a different and higher perspective.

You may have to deal with panic attacks and other mental or emotional disorders related to fear and anxiety. This, too, may require expert professional help. A person with these conditions must be helped, not punished for being weak or crazy.

Avoid being manipulated into making a sacrifice that will trap you into the role of victim. Avoid being and dating a martyr. Don't hang on to a relationship that is over or make yourself crazy because you are afraid of abandonment. That is not true love.

13. **DEATH**
TRANSFORMATION

UPRIGHT: No, start again.

The ghostly figure tries to run from DEATH but signs of disintegration are obvious. The DEATH card is not about physical death. Upright or reversed it means there is almost no hope that any situation you have asked about can be saved or an old situation resurrected. The fact that the card is upright means you will come to terms with this new reality.

Facing profound change is unpleasant but helps you realize what is important. As sad as it is, all things must pass away to make way for new growth in our spiritual development. It is not easy—passion, deep emotional ups and downs, and sexual magnetism are all pulling at your heartstrings now.

You will have to transform yourself in order to begin again. You must put the past in the past and believe you can find love again. Keep silent regarding what you've asked about. Don't speak about old relationships or even old times. Concentrate on what's happening now and what may be. Appreciate all the good things in your life and look to a new tomorrow. Hope never dies unless we let it die.

What is passing away served as a catalyst for transformation in your life. Karmically, you were helped to open new doors that you may have otherwise overlooked. As the poet Alfred Lord Tennyson said, "'Tis better to have loved and lost than never to have loved at all."

REVERSED: No.

DEATH reversed does not indicate that anyone is going to die. It indicates that there has been a failure to make major adjustments to give new life to a relationship and this stagnation has provoked serious consequences that are now coming to a head.

Like it or not, forces beyond your control are going to compel you to end something you would prefer not to end. If this is the case, you will not be given a second chance or a choice. You will be forced to cope with the loss of a relationship or the opportunity to create one and this profound transformation will be one you didn't prepare for or expect. Don't struggle in a bitter battle because your relationship, ultimately, will not survive.

The basic problem here is that you may not be able to let something go to make room for something new. Resisting change can be painful and it would be best if you let go and let God/dess guide you. However, it is more than likely you are going to have to obtain help to pick up the pieces of this relationship. This big transformation will be scary and will require difficult decisions. But if you try to resist the changes, you will repress emotions, stress, and sexual urges that will emerge inappropriately and at the worst possible times. It may take professional counseling to help you deal with this situation.

14. TEMPERANCE
PATIENCE

UPRIGHT: Yes, if you are patient.

A woman stands motionless, carefully balancing a paper lantern at the end of a stick, hoping to attract a golden bird to the seeds she has placed inside it. This scene symbolizes the qualities necessary to attract good fortune or good relationships: be still, balanced, and patient.

If you were going to say or do something important and that might have significant effect on your love life, drawing TEMPERANCE upright is an indication that you should wait until a more auspicious time. Now is not the time to be impetuous.

If you are without a partner, the upright TEMPERANCE card means relax, be patient, things are good. Letting things happen in their own time is an essential step on the road to your spiritual development, and remember—another meaning of TEMPERANCE—it is your spiritual development that is going to bring you true love. Wait a little longer for that certain person to make contact.

Let complexity work for you. Whatever you do, don't rush it. Do it at the perfect moment. Learn how others timed their plan and emulate them.

If you are in a relationship, things are going to work out for the best when you, your partner, or both of you are willing to be more patient and accepting, two attributes of true love. Channel your energy privately into making plans and making lists about what you want and don't want. The results of your planning may surprise you.

REVERSED: Maybe, if you are patient.

TEMPERANCE reversed shows the seeds falling out of the lantern, allowing the bird to eat them before the woman is ready. There's either been too much patience and planning regarding your love life or not enough. The issue of time and timing might be further complicating an overly complex situation.

Are you being so impatient that you're hurting yourself and your chance for true love? You don't have to wait forever, but give things a chance to evolve a bit before acting out.

Make sure that you or those with influence on you don't have a list of predetermined requirements about you and your ideal partner or relationship. This list of "must haves" and "can't live withs" may be keeping you from happiness with someone who's right for you—someone who, unlike you, is willing to compromise about your attributes.

TEMPERANCE reversed may also mean that you're too complacent about some aspect of what it takes to find, keep, and maintain true love, thinking it will take care of itself when, in truth, it needs you to take action. There is a difference between the patience that the TEMPERANCE card symbolizes and laziness and apathy or, in the extreme, depression.

Time and timing can manifest as problems in a few ways. In love affairs, everything will not come to those who wait and especially to those who wait too long. Age may be a problem. Being punctual is important, a sign of respect for those you're meeting.

15. THE DEVIL
SEDUCTION

UPRIGHT: No, be careful!

The beautiful Indian woman dancing with her snake clearly reveals the age-old association of the concept of THE DEVIL with seduction, temptation, and desire, sexual and otherwise. However, it is insulting to the whole human race, born from sexual encounters, for anyone to assign an inherently D-evil (sic) meaning to sex and everything associated with it.

If you have desired to initiate and/or experience more seductive and sexy behavior, the appearance of THE DEVIL is an indication that you are soon going to get your wish. You can think, act, and even dress a bit more seductively to obtain the kind of relationship that you have asked about. On occasion we all need to be seduced a bit to help us out of any limiting habits and patterns of behavior in which we have become trapped, but be careful!

THE DEVIL symbolizes excesses of every kind, and you may find yourself taking in and otherwise experiencing more than you were expecting. When you meet THE DEVIL, bring your moral compass—you are going to need it! You may have to "wear a mask" and "play the game," so keep secrets and don't volunteer information. You may even have to fib, and you should assume your partner is doing the same. Your will power is stronger than your desires, but only when you remember you have a choice and use it.

REVERSED: No! Be very, very careful!!

THE DEVIL card reversed shows the woman's leg loosely encircled by the snake's tail, a subtle variation on the rope cinched tightly around the ankle of THE HANGED MAN (12). This symbolizes that we are not held captives by our desires and appetites unless we allow this to become our experience, either through our beliefs, our actions, or our inaction.

Carefully examine the question you have asked—why did you ask it? THE DEVIL symbolizes the seduction of the material world. You may be contemplating a relationship that is mainly about money, power, status, appearances, and/or sex. This doesn't qualify as true love in our book.

You may have to mask your real intentions. Act with subtlety or do not act at all. You or your partner may be cheating or your relationship otherwise tested by lust, trickery, and greed. Someone may be lying to you or trying to seduce you with lies and trickery. It may also mean that person is lying to himself or herself and not to you—or you may be lying to yourself. The truth will soon be revealed.

You may be physically attracted to someone who is not worthy of you, who is simply using you for gratification, or is actually a threat to your health and safety. If a sexual encounter has already taken place then you may want to consult a health professional to make sure there are no lingering consequences to be concerned about.

16. THE TOWER
CRISIS

UPRIGHT: Yes, if you want to upset everyone.

Expect the unexpected. The collapsing tower of the burning building is an unpleasant reminder that nothing lasts forever. Even something that is built to last can meet an untimely end—including a relationship—when violent, unpredictable, and volatile energies are suddenly released. What replaces it—either an abandoned, ruble-strewn vacant lot or something new and beautiful you build to take its place—is up to you.

If you are in a relationship, the best you can expect is that it is going to change radically and for the better. If you've kept your relationship fresh and exciting, you have nothing to worry about. However, THE TOWER very often indicates sudden upsets so if you've been happy with the status quo, you're going to be disappointed.

If you've been praying for more freedom or some kind of fundamental restructuring of your relationship, including breaking up or divorcing, your prayers are about to be answered. Whatever happens next will not occur in the way you expected it to happen so prepare for big changes.

If you are looking for love, be careful. THE TOWER can portend that you are about to meet an unpredictable, rebellious, and disruptive type of person. If you like that type and are able to protect yourself from that person's craziness, then this is good news. THE TOWER can also predict that the person you've asked about is unstable in some way, possibly dangerous, and definitely not the faithful kind!

REVERSED: No!

THE TOWER reversed resembles a rocket taking off in an uncontrollable fashion, symbolizing that you may not be able to cope with the sudden release of energies that is about to happen. It may also indicate that the lack of progress, hope, or maybe just plain boredom is seriously threatening your love life. Whether you are looking for love or are in a relationship that seems to have gone stale, if you (or your partner) resist bringing newness into your love life, the pent-up energies of repressed desires and unspoken feelings will explode at the worst possible time and in the worst possible way.

THE TOWER reversed can also symbolize either you or the person you're interested in may feel so desperate about something that you are willing to upset everything and everyone to end your crisis. This kind of volatile, selfish behavior can start to manifest as innocent nervous energy, but suddenly escalate dramatically, seemingly out of nowhere.

Any problems you find yourself experiencing regarding the question you have asked may be the result of your or your love interest's lingering psychological problems, results of past upsets that proved how unreliable people, relationships, or simply life can be.

If you are lucky and THE TOWER reversed manifests as your encountering instability, revolutionary ideas, or the breakdown of established structures that show you the old rules no longer apply, then you may find yourself liberated in some way.

17. THE STAR
HOPE

UPRIGHT: Yes! Yes!

The storm clouds have parted, and a magical STAR has appeared in the sky as if in answer to the summons of a strong woman's trumpet blast. It shines so brightly and powerfully that the sun and the moon seem earthbound in comparison.

If you're looking for love, you may be about to meet the most wonderful person you've ever met—someone who stands out from the crowd. If you're with someone and things have been difficult, take heart! Either your relationship is about to undergo a period of profound healing or you're going to meet that wonderful new person!

This card indicates you should be very optimistic, even though you may have been burned in the past. You can see through phoniness and can assess character and underlying motives with clear perception. You can go back to being a hopeful and trusting person who values those traits in others.

You need to be the star of your show and experience a time of joy, wonder, hope, and healing. Calm down and re-establish your connection with your body. If you learn about the benefits of relaxation and rejuvenation and the illumination of spiritual realities, divine grace and spiritual harmony will soon be yours. Daydream about true love and balance that with practical action and your dreams will come true. THE STAR will help you manifest the trusting, nurturing, and fulfilling relationship that will bring you lasting joy and happiness.

REVERSED: Maybe, if you're up for it.

The sun and moon on THE STAR reversed have returned to the sky, symbolizing that you and/or your partner are now seen to be more human and less extraordinary than in the past. This is a natural part of the development of all relationships and dealing with it can make you and your relationship stronger.

You may not have felt like a star lately, and you need and deserve a time for healing. You might feel that you have to find your way on the true-love path without knowing who to trust or who to believe. You may feel uncharacteristically pessimistic, and it has affected your self-confidence. You may lack faith in yourself because lovers and friends have let you down. You've lowered your expectations. Disillusionment has replaced a formerly hopeful attitude.

Getting caught up in criticism and spite only creates doubt that a healthy and successful relationship can exist for you. You or someone you care about may now seem very cautious, reluctant to make a commitment. It may appear that you or your partner focus more on mistakes or broken promises than on finding ways to heal the problems.

You may hesitate to get involved in a relationship and be cynical about new possibilities and opportunities for true love because of past disappointment. Try not focusing so much on your hurt and unfulfilled dreams—it weakens your chances for improvements in the future.

18. THE MOON
FEAR

UPRIGHT: Maybe, but you never know.

Under a stern, seemingly disinterested MOON, a youthful figure wistfully cradles a ripe seed pod while a cat digs a hole in the earth to plant it. This scene symbolizes our sweet, noble efforts to cope with the shadow side of human existence, the doubts and fears about life and its meaning, and the depression that can arise when our emotions about our future overwhelm our ability to enjoy the present moment.

You do not have to fear the unknown. Depend on faith, intuition, and benevolent forces to lead you to true love. Get in touch with your dreams. You need to go forward, even without a clear picture of where you are, where you are going, or where you have been.

If shyness, insecurities, or depression are interfering in your quest for true love, find ways to cope. Breathing, meditating, and massage are all methods that can help you contact your higher self.

Become aware of what is going on in your inner world. Maternal instincts or issues with motherhood may come into play now. Reviewing family history and past partnerships will allow you react properly now. Make your home a place where you feel secure and supported. Otherwise, you will be overly sensitive and will act inappropriately as your moods shift and change with the cycles of the moon. Be alert to the fact that your dream lover also changes, and no relationship is always a dream come true.

REVERSED: No.

The image of THE MOON reversed shows the youthful figure hurtling toward THE MOON, symbolizing that efforts have failed to escape the moodiness and depression that accompanies a lack of emotional intelligence.

You may encounter darkness, fear, or confusion. You will be challenged to go on without a clear picture of the past, present, or future. Without intuition and faith in yourself and a higher power, you will not succeed. Your lack of clarity may be misleading others. Your unreasonable expectations may make you irrational or obsessive about a relationship. If you are unsure of yourself, develop awareness of your deep-seated fears about giving and receiving love.

You may be fantasizing about a relationship, thinking someone is "the one" before you even have a chance to appraise their true nature. You may choose to blind yourself to the warning signs of a relationship that is not meant to be.

You may feel overwhelmed by shyness or melancholy because your sensitive personality makes you feel too vulnerable and hurt. You may be moody—inspired one moment and then totally unmotivated the next. If you feel this way, it is better to withdraw until your mood improves than to go out and be known as a negative person. Things have to shift and change before they get better.

THE MOON reversed brings illusion and veiled intentions, but it also brings a truth that only the strongest can bear: finding true love does not solve all your other problems.

19. THE SUN
SUPPORT

UPRIGHT: Yes, enjoy yourself!

THE SUN has enough light and power for everyone, especially for the solar-powered wings of the wise scientist who has figured out how all people can fly. In ancient times, the sun was worshipped as a god but today we know that it is "just" a star. In the tarot THE SUN is supreme because it is a star that shines for all of us while THE STAR shows that we are each special in our individuality.

A positive attitude will attract others to you. THE SUN is one of the most positive tarot cards in the deck. You will soon be flying to your destiny date with true love—maybe to a sunny tropical isle! Flirty fun, play, and romance are all indicated. There will be fun get-togethers with family, friends, and lovers. You will have an inspired and intimate relationship based on true love and friendship.

You need to share your highest qualities and achievements. Radiate who you are and what you are doing always and all ways. Shine love on those you care about. You may be attracted to a strong, paternal figure. Support all efforts of a loved one to grow.

Someone is attracted to you and feels a special cosmic connection and soul response. You both can be nonjudgmental, respectful, and comfortable with each other. Friendship will be a valuable asset to this relationship. Existing relationships will improve dramatically when THE SUN shines his grace upon them.

REVERSED: Yes, but not as strong.

The winged flyer on THE SUN reversed has gotten too close to what he thought was a god and found it to be a fiery star that has melted his soar-powered wings.

You will enter a period of uneasiness about a relationship. You may feel that you cannot show your real feelings. Love, friendships, or gifts may disappoint. You or your partner may desire more attention, more money, or more power and cannot stop complaining. The good things in life may be overlooked.

Selfishness could be getting in the way of true love. You or a love interest may believe that they should be getting more than they are out of the relationship. There may be lingering regrets or unrealized dreams that prevent a happy and enduring compatibility. There will not be the contentment that you desire. You cannot be happy with anyone else unless you are happy with yourself.

If you have not spent time developing a sense of independence and self-sufficiency, you will be uncertain of what direction to go. A parent might be putting pressure on you or there may be other demands that make you feel inadequate to the task at hand.

You may feel that you cannot spend enough time on your creativity. Family will be more unpredictable than ever and may try to influence your relationship. You may want to go to a warm or sunny climate, but your plans will be disrupted or put on hold.

20. JUDGMENT
PERSPECTIVE

UPRIGHT: Yes, if you rise above the situation.

The woman floating over the city in the JUDGMENT card upright symbolizes that if you want true love, you need to rise above pettiness, blame, and guilt to gain a clear perspective on your situation. Don't give up! A time of reckoning brings the end of your quest for true love near. It may even come in the form of the resurrection of a former love affair.

If you've been without a partner, know that you will have a relationship in a relatively short time if you do not settle for less than you deserve. Judge potential partners by what you know now about yourself and your needs, not by what you used to want. Stand up for yourself and your right to judge—don't be politically correct about vital issues.

By reviewing what you've been through together, the good and the bad, an existing relationship will be revitalized. Kindness and the desire to improve will prevail, leading to the resurrection of love and attraction once thought dead. Each partner will take responsibility for past mistakes and rebuild a trust and bond with each other. If an aspect of your relationship ends, that ending will also be a beginning.

Face your past without fear now. JUDGMENT upright can also mean that you will win a judgment against you or give up a bad habit and rise to the occasion to save a marriage or a close relationship. Avoid harsh judgments, especially about yourself.

REVERSED: No, your judgment is off.

Prepare for a time of reckoning when accounts are settled and past karma is balanced. You or your relationship will be judged and may be found wanting. Even if you are not judged by another, your inner critic may get the best of you, causing you to judge yourself or your partner too harshly. Expect shifting emotions in yourself and others, especially if there is a refusal to awaken to what is real.

In an existing relationship there may not be enough love, kindness, or resources to get you through a dark time. A past love or lover may complicate the picture. If there has been deceit or laziness, then surprising revelations will occur and threaten to end your relationship.

If you don't have a committed relationship, be careful before you turn a new friendship into a love connection. Someone may not be willing to match the other's efforts for self-improvement. You may have to be blunt to create awareness and progress. If you are trying to save a relationship, don't play the blame game. You may feel like getting revenge, but that will only delay your recovery.

The JUDGMENT card reversed is a warning to face the facts and confront the past and its demons and shadows in yourself or a love interest. Plans may not be realized as hoped. Or you may be hanging onto a frustrating, unhappy situation when you should give up. Forgive, starting with yourself, or you won't be forgiven.

UPRIGHT: Yes! You've done well!

Graduation time! Promises will be kept and your deepest desires will soon be fulfilled. A major milestone will be reached. You will soon attain a degree of achievement and understanding that rewards you in a physical, mental, and spiritual nature for your efforts to find true love and/or improve your existing relationship.

If you haven't yet met your mate, now is the time for the perfect relationship to flow to you naturally, maybe in the form of someone from a different country, race, or ethnic background. Respect cultural differences but don't sacrifice or sublimate your own because true love never requires such a thing. You have finally come to know yourself so be yourself always and in all ways.

The angel's trumpet symbolizes that you should announce your love to the world. It is a perfect time to exchange gifts and have a party, especially one where you can dress up and dance the night away. Say yes to marriage and announce your engagement. Partnered or not, this rare time of culmination must be identified and honored with gifts and celebrations.

A long cycle has ended and a new cycle is about to begin. It is a potent time to set your intention to make your new dreams, based on your new situation, a reality. Throw off old habits that have outlived their usefulness and open your eyes and ears to wonderful opportunities and exciting discoveries. You may want to travel and see the world.

REVERSED: Maybe, if you act like a grown-up.

The angel guarding Earth symbolizes that the world, its people, and your love interests do not owe you anything. You have to raise yourself up and earn what you want and that takes work, starting with working on yourself and especially your spiritual development.

Don't make a big deal out of the state of your love life in conversation with third parties. Your secrets might be shared. And there may be problems caused by the level of education, social graces, and worldly sophistication—or lack of them—possessed by you, your partner, or both of you.

If you are looking for love be careful not to get involved with someone whose nationality, beliefs, or background is so different from yours that it creates insurmountable barriers to your sharing true love. Lovers want to give each other a world of love, light, and laughter, not force their partner into a world of restrictions.

Even though an important cycle of your love life is ending and there are still many lessons to be learned it could be difficult to focus now because your confidence is weakened. This is not the time to say yes to marriage, travel, or any other commitments. Promises may not be kept. Old feelings of unrequited love or co-dependency may crop up. You must leave inappropriate behavior and habits behind, or you will not graduate to the next level of your relationship or find true love in the world.

THE COURT CARDS AND THE MINOR ARCANA

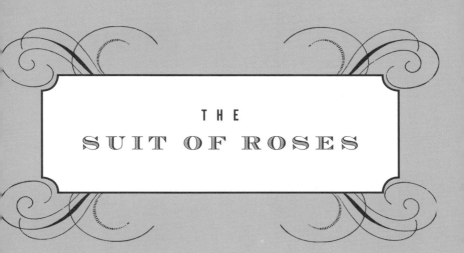

THE
SUIT OF ROSES

PRINCESS OF ROSES
THE ADVENTURER

UPRIGHT: Yes.

The PRINCESS OF ROSES impetuously picked up a wand in either hand, though she is not yet skilled enough to wield them even one at a time. Her enthusiasm makes up for her lack of experience, however, and she will make good use of her new tools as she gains valuable experience.

You will encounter or have to act like a young or young-looking, fun, enthusiastic woman. You need to be positive and spontaneous—kiss your sweetheart, take a weekend trip, laugh and tell jokes. Lighten up. Remember, your actions speak louder than your words. The lessons you learn about love now will last you a lifetime. If you want to get someone interested, be upbeat and ready for action.

A busy, energetic young woman may bring a new acquaintance into your life. When you meet this person, throw yourself into the relationship with innocent abandon and an open heart. You may have the urge to jump into a new relationship or suddenly walk away from an existing one. Go for it!

This card can also mean that your own youthful, romantic spirit captivates those around you. As you experiment and grow and come to better understand your social skills and the laws of attraction, you will also learn about emotional needs in yourself and those you care about. Go on an adventure, work out, or play outdoors with each other, your pets, and/or your friends who have pets. Have fun inventing and using "pet" names for each other.

REVERSED: Maybe.

The PRINCESS OF ROSES impetuously picked up a wand in either hand, though she was not yet skilled enough to wield them even one at a time. Her good intentions and enthusiasm didn't make up for her lack of experience.

Be careful if you encounter someone who looks, acts, or dresses wild, flamboyant, or too young. Make sure that person is not you—that and impulsive, immature acts will drive away potential partners. Don't get ahead of yourself. Trying to move a relationship too quickly will scare someone with less fire in his or her personality. Avoid tactlessness, anger, and childish theatrics if you don't get your way.

Be careful how you create and use "pet" names for your partner and keep them private. You or your partner may skip from one relationship to the next, seeking the "perfect" one. Problems can arise if boredom sets in or if one or both of you give up at the first sign of trouble. It can't always be a party. True love has a serious side too. Don't run away from doing the work of having a relationship. Ask a mature friend for words of wisdom about your current situation to ensure you are not being naïve. Social skills must be developed. If you and/or your partner change your ways, you'll be rewarded with a great relationship. Don't change and you'll waste time doing too much of the wrong things, making promises you can't keep, and socializing with the wrong crowd.

PRINCE OF ROSES
THE MOVER

UPRIGHT: Yes.

The PRINCE OF ROSES has bred a completely new species of rose and dedicated it to his true love. He is a competitive young man who attracts excitement. He is brave and honest and likes to shake things up. He is a risk-taker who loves the thrill of the chase and moves in quickly to get hot and heavy. He likes to win. His tendency is to go on to the next conquest without waiting around for a relationship to grow.

You are about to meet or be required to take on the role of a person with the qualities of the PRINCE OF ROSES. An enthusiastic, open-minded partner may soon be yours. A person such as this brings fresh energy into your life but can also wear you out with his or her challenging behavior. This card can also indicate that your love life will be improved by movement such as a journey, a promotion, or a change of residence. Promotion can also mean getting publicity or even the "buzz" of favorable gossip—all of these things can help your relationships now.

Don't be shy or ashamed about who you are and where you've come from. Be proud of yourself and your reputation. Be a pioneer in the choices you make. Be an original.

This card is the green light for developing some venture on your own. Take calculated risks in your relationships and don't overanalyze why or how things are working. Don't look back. It is time to try fresh, trendy things and spend time with new people who will stimulate you.

REVERSED: Maybe.

The PRINCE OF ROSES has transplanted his prized flower one too many times and is now worried it may die. This card reversed indicates you must be careful about wanting to improve someone "for your own good." You can't change anyone else—it's hard enough to change oneself!

You and your partner are not on the same page concerning future plans. Now is not the right time to force things, especially a journey, a change of residence, or improving your position. In particular, moving can incite irritability and quarrels with your friends and family. Stay calm if a younger person around you starts bragging, fighting, or otherwise acting irrationally.

If you are feeling bored and in need of more passion or adventure in your love life, someone may come and try to sweep you off your feet. Have fun but don't expect too much in return. Be careful about getting involved too quickly, especially with a bullying type who attracts you with his ardent interest. He may be one who "loves 'em and leaves 'em."

This is not the best time to confront a partner directly about working to improve your relationship. What comes to the surface might prove unpleasant and have lasting negative consequences, especially from long-repressed, half-baked notions spoken in haste and regretted just as fast. Keep thoughts and ambitions to yourself now or malicious gossip will damage your reputation.

QUEEN OF ROSES
THE LEADER

UPRIGHT: Yes.

The QUEEN OF ROSES is as skilled at attracting people to her and managing the intrigue that swirls around her court as the spiders who've woven diamond-shaped webs in tribute to her. She is magnetic and creative. She knows everyone and their secrets and knows how to use information to make things happen. She is popular and fiercely independent.

When you emulate and/or get involved with someone with her energy and qualities it will generate possibilities for an active social life. She is willful and likes excitement and attention. She always wants to meet new people, and she will pull you along with her. If she is with a partner she will push and prod that person to play and have more fun. She is cheerful, and those around her feel the warmth, love, and humor from her sunny disposition. She can tire you out with her busy schedule and can-do attitude.

Feel inspired and you will inspire trust. Push yourself to be positive and self-assured. Behave like royalty. Use your connections to get things done. Be true to your beliefs about true love and it will manifest in your life.

Heat up your romantic life by being more outgoing. Parties and other gatherings will benefit you. Find a project that stimulates you—it will lead you to meet like-minded people. Inspire with your enthusiasm and vitality. Don't worry about what others think.

REVERSED: Maybe.

The QUEEN OF ROSES has become entangled in the spider webs of her garden even though she knew they were there and thought she knew well how to avoid them. She has come to depend on others too much and is unable to free herself with her own efforts.

You will either encounter a person who seems insecure or irresponsible when it comes to love and sexual liaisons or have to face the fact that you are or have been behaving this way. The person may act like a sexy, charismatic, self-assured individual who knows how things must be done, but inside feels powerless and frustrated. She may put on a good act but, in reality, is sick about an unfortunate love situation. She stirs up anger and jealousy by being competitive and confrontational.

This person wants to be thought of as an authority. To be a good leader, however, you have to consider the needs of others. Do not use your charisma and leadership abilities exclusively to further your own interests. You'll not find true love if you do.

You may come across a situation, cause, or creative project that becomes a competition or power struggle. Your rival may come in the form of a narcissist or someone with a superiority complex, but she is afraid of her own shadow. You may feel pushed by a love interest to achieve more than you are presently seeking. You may grow to resent that he or she is not satisfied with your drive or ambition.

KING OF ROSES
THE MOTIVATOR

UPRIGHT: Yes.

The KING OF ROSES seems distracted. The several dark branches emanating from behind his crown, however, symbolize he earned his kingdom because of the way he can expertly manage several projects at the same time.

You are soon either going to meet or be called upon to be a person displaying the qualities of the KING OF ROSES. He exudes the best traits of maturity without the complaints, regrets, and slowness of age. He has a great personality—he is good-natured and very interested in others—though he is not overly intellectual. He is a doer, not a thinker. He is a motivator, and his control, confidence, and intense honesty lead you to accept his opinions. He is used to being the leader and being in a position of command.

Be a great king and think about and confront your own strengths and weaknesses. Once they are clearly seen you can use this self-knowledge to your advantage. A truly scientific, mathematical approach will work best. Try making a detailed, map-like plan of all the relationship dynamics involved in your situation. Then act with passion and decisiveness to get your way.

Loyalty will be shown to you now and your loyalty will be rewarded. You will manifest your dream of true love, and quite soon. You can fall in love fast now because this dynamic person opens the door to many possibilities for a better situation than you have experienced in the past.

REVERSED: Maybe.

The KING OF ROSES reversed is distracted. His crown is caught on the several dark branches behind him, symbolizing that he cannot manage his kingdom properly because there are so many projects going on at the same time.

Be careful not to gamble or take on too much now—you may lose. You will most likely encounter a domineering person who is absolutely certain he or she is right—make sure this person is not you. This is someone who likes to talk only about himself. He can be crude. Meanness, pettiness, and cheapness are all issues to address and deal with. The tenderness you crave in a relationship may be missing.

This card reversed can indicate disloyalty and someone with multiple relationships. An ego problem or spiritual pride, either in you or another, can block true love. Beware the tendency to give up power because it is "spiritual" or because this is what the other person wants. Either way it is not healthy.

You may be impressed with a person who seems to have everything going his or her way but is actually in bad shape. He or she is not ready to get involved the way you would like and cannot or will not give wholly to a relationship. THE KING OF ROSES reversed can also indicate that a clash of attitudes regarding politics, sports, entertainment, and technology use may cause problems in your relationship.

ACE OF ROSES
PASSION

UPRIGHT: Yes!

An exciting breakthrough in personal relationships occurs, maybe even a new opportunity for romance! One of you considers the other person "the one!" You and/or the person who lights your fire are feeling positive, self-confident, affectionate, and sexy. There are new prospects for improvement in an existing relationship. This is a time of initiation and originality. Go on first impulses and impressions. Make the first move. Flirt! If you're sure it's right, signal your desires to a special someone. Don't hold back. You will be rewarded if you make new friends or help an existing relationship.

REVERSED: Yes.

Action is initiated but it doesn't go well. Someone you're not that into may be overly interested in you. Or you may embarrass yourself by moving too far too fast with someone who's just not into you. A new beginning or breakthrough in a relationship is delayed by lack of trust, honesty, or maybe just energy. There is a need for more intimacy, passion, and little displays of affection. More faith is needed or there will be frustration and worry. Be careful not to jump to conclusions or overreact. Finger-pointing arguments could be ignited resulting in an emotional meltdown.

TWO OF ROSES
CROSSROADS

UPRIGHT: Yes and no.

Things are at a crossroads but you're in a position of power. You can make, break, or even take a relationship away from someone. But take a time-out before you act. Planning is more important than taking action now. Contemplate where you are, where you've been, where you want to go, and with whom. Someone feels two ways about his or her partner or may think he or she is in love with two different people. If that's you, don't decide now. Keep both relationships going. Prepare for intimate conversations about commitment and sexual relations and you won't be worried about unintended consequences.

REVERSED: No and maybe.

You are at a crossroads so take care. Plans must be updated when things change. Lack of planning can cause mistrust and loss of faith. Establish your emotional equilibrium before taking action. Don't make too many decisions at once. Avoid the tendency to blame and find fault. The misuse of criticism can thwart your plans for happiness, reconciliation, or for the deepening of an early-stage relationship. Be careful of actions taken that are at cross-purposes and/or self-defeating. Get out of your own way. Don't be scattered or ambivalent. Poor planning can cause much confusion.

THREE OF ROSES
OPPORTUNITY

UPRIGHT: Yes!

Allow yourself to feel happy and upbeat, with or without a reason. Try to be open, uninhibited, and adventurous, even if you are shy. Use your connections, network and call in favors. You need to become more aware of opportunities to improve your love life and/or relationships. More people than you are aware of are attracted to you. Someone may leave the person they are with to be with you and it will work out well. You may find an opportunity for romance with someone you have never thought about in that way. You may even have to find a way to balance more than one relationship!

REVERSED: Yes.

A wonderful opportunity may be missed or squandered. An existing partner or a new person may be not valued properly or may be overlooked entirely. Be faithful to a deserving partner. If the relationship in question triangulates, it will not go well. Put your partner ahead of your friends, family, or even children, or pay the consequences. Broadening your knowledge about the world and its people can help you avoid missteps. Don't be passive. Seize the day. Resolution may not come soon or easily. Don't waste time with people who do not take responsibility for their own actions—and don't be one!

FOUR OF ROSES
RESPECT

UPRIGHT: Yes!

This card is an indication of a long and happy marriage. An existing relationship or one you are about to establish soon will be blessed by longevity, as well as by love, gratitude, and respect given and received in equal measure. This card is a very good omen for a wedding or engagement. It can also indicate that an important date is approaching. Appropriate words, gifts, and other tokens of appreciation should be exchanged to honor what you have worked hard to accomplish. If you are not ready to marry, then have a party or otherwise share your good fortune with those you care about.

REVERSED: Yes.

Don't try to move your relationship along faster than you should. Avoid talking about spending your lives together. You would be better off working on developing friendship and a more positive attitude. There is too much fear about the future. Compulsive behaviors can interfere with trust and commitment. Hostility can keep you from the completion of an important course of action. It may seem that your hard work on a relationship will not pay off. Friends that you expect to come through for you may not. Don't over-analyze the situation. Let go of internalized resentments and get to work.

FIVE OF ROSES
COMPETITION

UPRIGHT: Maybe.

Being tactful and considerate rather than confrontational is usually the best way to have better communication and deeper intimacy in your relationship. However, you must face the fact that you are in competition with another in your search for true love. To overcome it can help you experience what teamwork really means and requires. Respect your opponent, but stand up for your point of view. Refuse to be a victim by voicing your opinions clearly. There may be control issues, so don't let a little quarrel turn into a tense, competitive fight. Try to stay patient and centered even if you suspect betrayal.

REVERSED: No.

The competition is quite fierce and powerful forces arrayed against you may be too much to overcome at this time. Gossip, jealousy, or insensitivity may drive you to an argument that you might regret. A misunderstanding may lead to a decrease in your self-esteem. Someone's inconsiderate actions can unleash pent-up emotions. Be careful not to let a disagreement about a small matter overly upset you. Guard against actions based on frustration, anger, hate, and prejudice. If you suspect disloyalty, take a breather before you have a confrontation, as the information you are acting on may not be true.

SIX OF ROSES
VICTORY

UPRIGHT: Yes!

Victory! You are a winner! If you've asked about another person, he or she is wonderful! Your victory will last longer if you really want what you are going for. Share your success with a loved one and position yourself for the next blaze of glory. It may involve a big party or celebration. The spotlight will be on you, so appreciate this happy time. You are feeling charismatic and ready to make important decisions about your future, but keep in mind that others involved may not be feeling so worthy. Be sensitive to their feelings and know that your path to success has made you a more caring person.

REVERSED: Yes.

You may not get what you think you need or want to have happen now. A setback will occur if you have been thinking only about your own needs. Contemplating past losses can help you prepare for future challenges. Someone may be using flattery or manipulation to win your favor so beware of phonies. You may feel so overly dependent on another that you believe you cannot stand on your own two feet. Do not allow this dependency to lead you to take an action you should not, one based on old patterns of self-sabotaging behavior.

SEVEN OF ROSES
COURAGE

UPRIGHT: Yes!

You and/or a partner will display true heroism. There will be enough courage to overcome fears and create true love. You need to lovingly articulate what you are aiming for in a relationship. There is an important and necessary action you must take now to know what true courage means. You set your boundaries, but then come out from behind your defenses and go forward with your plans in spite of your fears. Use your creative energies for resolving conflicts. Patience in the face of difficulties will pay off. Don't be afraid to stand up for yourself. Do not compromise, waiver, or give up.

REVERSED: Maybe.

You need to summon all your courage to go forward. You may have to fight the urge to give up on a person, a relationship, or a dream. Fears about commitment are your main adversary now. Feeling overwhelmed, you may retreat rather than deal with your hurt and abandonment issues. Be willing to go it alone if you have to. Do not assert yourself too much now, or your actions will lead to an embarrassing situation. Defensive behavior with the person you love only creates more confusion. If hot tempers flare, you may not have the confidence to straighten things out quickly enough.

EIGHT OF ROSES
SIGNALS

UPRIGHT: Yes!
The energy and love you have been putting out comes back to you in a very positive way. Someone tells you they love you or vice versa. A beautiful love affair is initiated, sustained, or improved via computer, e-mail, telephone, postal letter, or any other means of communication. You may be feeling very tuned in to a wonderful person. If so, take action and make your intentions perfectly clear. Pay attention to signs and symbols—including body language—they're as important as words. Make plans now, not later. Live your lives together in your own unique way and follow your bliss.

REVERSED: Yes.
Communication problems may interfere with your love life. Your intentions might be misunderstood. Plans and directions may go awry. Messages of love, romance, and appreciation will be blocked. Communications will be missed— computer problems can cause lost e-mails, answering machines break, or phone calls or letters get lost or remain unanswered. Secrets could be revealed prematurely or past their time to have good effect. You may wonder if the other person ever really cared or meant what he or she said. You may fear that you have been taken for granted and start to resent all sorts of imagined slights.

NINE OF ROSES
HABITS

UPRIGHT: Yes.

To convert your longings for true love into a real, healthy relationship requires discipline and health. Your willpower, character, and body may soon be tested. Things will go well if you eat right, exercise, and strive to be healthy. Avoid anything or anyone that impairs your judgment and physical abilities. Don't do anything to excess. Avoid intoxication, including intoxicated and otherwise negative people, as well as dangerous areas. Learn and practice self-defense techniques now so you can confidently defend yourself and your lover. Stay faithful to your word and to your core beliefs.

REVERSED: Maybe.

Self-defeating habits threaten your relationship. Lack of discipline can cause you to let yourself go, sacrificing long-term goals for short-term pleasures. Too much discipline makes you so rigid you can't adapt to new information or acknowledge your needs. Someone will try to take advantage of you if you and/ or your partner become undisciplined or a slave to your habits. You may stay with a person or course of action when you shouldn't and/or feel you can't deal with the pressure and demands of your relationship. You may cancel important plans or give up too soon on a lover.

TEN OF ROSES
STRESS

UPRIGHT: No.

It is good you have the ability to persevere and concentrate, but it is possible you are working too hard. It may be interfering with the attention or affection others expect from you. If you cannot stop the demands of your work, then you must try to conserve your energy and pace yourself. When you are over-committed everything becomes a strain. Take little breathers and make time every day to let others know you love and care about them. You may be feeling trapped or restricted but delay making decisions about your relationships. Exhaustion will impede anyone's judgment.

REVERSED: No!

You will encounter stressful conditions. Overwork and responsibilities drain you and prevent clear thinking. Define your goals clearly or it will be difficult to carry the heavy load that is on your shoulders. You are over-committed, and your tendency may be to act out in a desperate way. It is a good time to share your burdens with a trusted advisor, as you may be expecting too much of yourself. There is a pattern from your past of being too rigid, controlling, or uncompromising, and that pattern has negatively affected some of your relationships. Stay in touch with those you care about.

THE
SUIT OF WINGS

PRINCESS OF WINGS
THE MESSENGER

UPRIGHT: Maybe.

The PRINCESS OF WINGS upright is an angel, a word derived from the Greek word angelos meaning "messenger." Her bird and butterfly companions also use their wings to spread the message of peace and beauty far and wide. Her seated posture and faraway look symbolizes that she is waiting to speak with you about your future.

You will encounter or have to act like a youthful, intelligent, versatile person who knows how to communicate. The purpose of this is to help an existing or future partner and you develop your ability to focus and gain insight and direction for valuable and meaningful idea(s). You will share many interests and talk and theorize together for hours. You may research with or for this person. You may seek knowledge together through books, classes, the Internet, or by traveling. You might meet a partner through the Internet or through a well-read and/or communicative friend.

Information will change your life. As you come to appreciate your original ideas more you may begin to put them into action. You and/or your partner will have the ability to see strengths and weaknesses in people, ideas, and designs. One of you may be or become a professional writer, communicator, or consultant. You may find yourself feeling very turned on romantically by intellectual stimulation. Keep a journal or write stories based on your life.

REVERSED: Maybe.

The PRINCESS OF WINGS is an angel, but she hasn't learned how to use her own set of wings correctly. She's flapping around too much and not getting anywhere, upsetting her bird and butterfly friends and causing them to take evasive measures.

Be careful if you encounter someone who looks, thinks, or communicates in a childish, sloppy, or eccentric way, and make sure that person is not you. Information, ideas, and abstract theories can get surprisingly mixed up and confused now, possibly because of a bright young person who is a bit unfocused—once again, is this you? This person gets into trouble by exaggerating and embellishing the truth and volunteering too much information. Close associates will be considered accomplices.

There is a good chance that you and/or your partner's words may pull you into a stormy battle of wits with each other or with others. Someone may be misinterpreting another person's signals, thinking they are suggesting a partnership when they are only teasing. The ability to be clear will be tested. Issues regarding gossip, privacy, discretion, and a big-mouthed young person may come back to haunt you.

Someone around you may be an idealist, which can also make him or her seem intolerant and disapproving. The person lacks the warmth to laugh off petty differences and may harshly judge you and your political or spiritual beliefs.

PRINCE OF WINGS
THE CHALLENGER

UPRIGHT: Maybe.

The PRINCE OF WINGS is upright in more ways than one. He strides forcefully through his father's kingdom, his sword drawn to defend it and all who live there, including his friends the butterflies and birds. This card symbolizes someone with strongly held beliefs, so strong that he or she is willing to fight and sacrifice for them.

You are about to meet or be required to take on the role of a person with the qualities of the PRINCE OF WINGS. Strong measures will be taken to turn ideas and ideals into reality. A curious person possessing a mind always seeking to expand and grow will be exciting and attractive. Clever, outspoken, and knowledgeable about current events, the stock market, and even pop culture, this person, who devours everything from data to trivia, is constantly entertaining and is a great resource for information. The search for insight and power of analysis would also be a turn-on to you and/or your partner.

Don't think about long-term commitments. Rethink your ideas about relationships. Your next step will soon become clear. It is crucial that you like someone for their mind, not their money or their looks, to be successful in love and career. This prince can help you get connected to what is best for your highest good and greatest joy. No need to hurry now, even though that might be your tendency. Try to be more reflective and you can reach your goals.

REVERSED: No.

The PRINCE OF WINGS reversed is striving to be upright, but his youthful desire to be right is stronger than his desire to live in harmony with those he seeks to help with his compelling ideas. He strides forcefully through his father's kingdom, his sword drawn to defend it and all who live there, including his friends the butterflies and birds, but he ends up pushing them out of the way and cutting himself with his own sword. Reversed, this card symbolizes someone with strongly held beliefs, so strong that he or she is willing to fight and sacrifice for them. The trouble is they might not be worth the degree of trouble caused by fighting for them—people could get hurt.

You are about to meet or be required to take on the role of a person with the qualities of the PRINCE OF WINGS. If you only fantasize but do not take the time to develop your skills, ingenuity, and self-esteem, frustration and defensiveness will cause you trouble. Be careful not to get dragged into a quarrel—you may not win this one even if you and/or your opponent likes a good fight. This person enjoys testing you, and acts like a cat with a mouse. You may have tense words with each other, a battle of wits.

You may fight over incompetence or bring work frustrations home that trigger dysfunctional behavior among family members. Watch for a destructive tendency to be fascinated by aggressive or otherwise eccentric types.

QUEEN OF WINGS
THE ANALYST

UPRIGHT: Maybe.

The unmarried QUEEN OF WINGS upright has shed the angel's wings she wore as a young princess. The barren tree behind her symbolizes that nothing in the world lasts forever. The butterfly on her forehead signifies she has transformed her thought processes in response to the events of her life.

When you emulate and/or get involved with someone with her qualities, the need to feel independent and self-sufficient is overwhelming. If not, you're better off alone. This card can symbolize that you and/or your partner is or was divorced, widowed, or single by choice and will stay only in a relationship characterized by this card's qualities of honesty, directness, and an understanding of all aspects of life, unclouded by sentimentality or superstition. To find this person, always think with your head not with your heart. Be direct. Express your understanding of life and its challenges. If you've suffered a lot, a wry wit can help reduce uneasiness.

You may meet or already know a private person who is precise, picky, and can't stand disorganization. This person is a great conversationalist and excellent listener and can give you wise advice as well as make you laugh. But this person is also shrewd and calculating when it comes to relationships and definite about what is right and wrong. Life's wounds have taught him or her emotional intelligence and crafted a good counselor and mentor.

REVERSED: No.

The unmarried QUEEN OF WINGS reversed has had the angel's wings she wore as a young princess taken away from her because she misused them. The upside-down tree behind her looks like roots symbolizing that barrenness is a big issue in her present life. She seems to be crushing the butterfly on her forehead, suggesting she resists transformation and the beauty it could bring into her life.

When you emulate and/or try to get involved with someone with the QUEEN OF WINGS qualities there is the danger that one or both of you need to feel totally independent and self-sufficient, an attitude that can doom the best relationships. You must face the fact that if you or your partner totally rejects the notion of positive change, you're better off alone. This card can indicate that you, your partner, or both are or were divorced, widowed, or single by choice, feel secure with it, and, therefore, may be frightened of the changes a relationship will bring.

The qualities of honesty and directness do not require that the sweet, sentimental, and spiritual side of life be avoided or persecuted. Pent-up bitterness may turn into malicious disregard for other people's feelings. Be careful loneliness does not turn strength into rigidity, tactlessness, or prudishness. Do not venture further into a relationship if there is no humor or mental stimulation. Avoid getting involved in a relationship where one or both of you are trying to work on the other for the other's own good.

KING OF WINGS
THE PROFESSIONAL

UPRIGHT: Yes.

The KING OF WINGS upright is even more upright than his princely son. He is a pillar of his community and has used his prodigious intellect and legendary wisdom in the writing and enforcement of its laws. He eschews a crown as being too pretentious and wears a hat adorned with souvenirs of his diplomatic visits to other realms.

You are soon either going to meet or be called upon to be a person displaying the qualities of the KING OF WINGS. This is a person who can use laws—both natural and manmade—diplomacy, history, common sense, and a broad understanding of human nature to solve problems or to get his or her way, but also possesses the wisdom to know what is best. Education and philosophical knowledge are important, but so are idle thoughts and daydreams.

When people get overly emotional this person is assertive, stays focused, and takes control. Relationships are second nature. A partner's judgment is valued and praised, even though it is done coolly or even assertively as if acknowledging a worthy debate opponent. But, still, this person is hard to resist. You both are free thinkers on the same wavelength, sharing your sharp philosophical insights. There is a definite chemistry between you. A quick mind and mature air of authority are very attractive features. When the KING OF WINGS upright appears prepare to meet a partner who is equally great as a teacher or a lover.

REVERSED: Maybe.

The KING OF WINGS reversed is more uptight than his driven princely son. Keeping up his image as a pillar of his community is a burden to him and the stress and strain is starting to show on his face and in his communications. He seems quite conflicted. His prodigious intellect is at odds with his legendary wisdom in the interpretation and enforcement of his laws, publicly as well as privately in his own family. He is overly concerned with other people's opinions, and political correctness makes his life difficult.

You are soon either going to meet or be called upon to change your ways if you see that you are a person displaying the qualities of the KING OF WINGS reversed. Education and philosophical knowledge are important, but idle thoughts and daydreams that lead to creative solutions may be undervalued.

This person can be inappropriately assertive and controlling out of habit. Relationships may be used to keep up appearances. He or she might have been through an unhappy divorce or a failed business venture. A partner's judgment may not be valued and praised.

Sometimes this card indicates a struggle with an important decision you just can't resolve. You or someone you are involved with may seem unfair and overly critical or arrogant about what you deserve. One or both of you may be living too much in your head and neglecting your health or physical needs.

ACE OF WINGS
TRIUMPH

UPRIGHT: Yes!

You have the right idea! Let it focus you and organize your life accordingly, and you will manifest the exact kind of relationship you want (as long as you don't get obsessive!). Keep thinking the way you've been thinking. Ask the important questions of everyone, especially of yourself. Let long-term goals and major principles enable you to make your relationships all they can be. You will have knowledge and the wisdom and willpower to apply it. Read a great self-help book and a brilliant new idea will reveal itself. Your life's unique purpose may even become crystal clear.

REVERSED: Maybe.

Blindly following an idea, plan, or person—even a good one—will cause trouble if new information is not allowed to inform decisions. Information or intellect used as a weapon to force things to go a certain way will backfire. Lies, adversity, and ignorance will undermine the genuine communication that true love requires. Asking too much of a person guarantees discontent. Cutting off a spiritual practice or person will cause anxiety. Fearing that your partner and/or you are not up to a challenge produces a self-fulfilling prophecy. If you are unsure about speaking your mind, be silent.

TWO OF WINGS
BALANCE

UPRIGHT: Maybe.
A postponement or taking a break will help your quest for true love. A new and different way to meet people will be surprisingly successful. Rest and relaxation are important to your love life. Balance work and play. A vacation can help you find true love. Alternative ideas and viewpoints must be discussed. Diplomacy and the desire for peace will benefit your relationships now. Being right is not as important as being kind and gentle. Give yourself permission to dream and look within. Yoga or meditation done with a partner can help harmonize your relationship as well as your mind and body.

REVERSED: Maybe.
A postponement may lead to neglect or outright abandonment. A real vacation is needed but cannot be taken yet, or a vacation could be disappointing—a mismatch between the dream and reality. Avoidance or procrastination could create a stalemate with a loved one. If you rest your mind and stop worrying, you can consider alternative ideas and viewpoints that will help create more balance in your relationships—even to the point of helping you find true love. Be more discriminating or you will get tangled in an unstable situation. A shallow or misleading person may try to make you doubt yourself.

THREE OF WINGS
SORROW

UPRIGHT: No.

You need to come to terms with an old hurt or broken heart. Not doing so may prevent the experience of a healthy relationship. Now is not the time to detach from your feelings but a good time to get in touch with your pain and sorrow. Though life is sometimes very sad, recovery can and will occur with time. It takes faith, self-love, and kindness. Count your blessings as you forgive yourself and others. Give yourself credit for endurance, as that will also help strengthen your resolve to make choices that honor your emotional needs. Peace begins when and where your expectations end.

REVERSED: No.

Your search for true love may be negatively affected by pain and sorrow in either yourself or another. Denying the sorrows of life can lead to loss, hostility, and disease. Defenses may be weakened by despair, and grief may threaten to overwhelm even the best intentions. Boundaries may be violated. Be careful of irrational behavior in yourself or others. They may accuse you of coldness or trying to control them. You may be uncomfortable with your role as a caregiver. Hardships make it difficult to find happiness now or to let go of your pain. Get professional help to deal with these issues.

FOUR OF WINGS
PRIVACY

UPRIGHT: Maybe.
Your love life can benefit now from seclusion and retreat from the pressures and demands of an active social life. Spend quiet time alone with your lover. Avoid confrontation. Taking a break from painful relationship issues, conflict, and distractions will help you rid yourself of stress and anxiety. Get back to your center by looking inward. For a real change, meditate or pray daily. Listen to your inner voice. Learn who you are now and with whom you have chosen to be involved. If you are looking for love, you can best find it in quiet, healing places and gentle, spiritual people.

REVERSED: Maybe.
If you are looking for love, anxiety caused by isolation and loneliness will prevent you from putting yourself into the places and situations where you can meet people. Problems in an existing relationship may be the result of one or both of you avoiding opening your heart to commitment because true love has the potential to cause true pain. You may feel impotent, unable to make real and necessary changes, as your energy has been drained by upsets. You may be reluctant to withdraw your attention from an unpleasant situation, but you must retreat from this limiting, though temporary, circumstance.

FIVE OF WINGS
DEFEAT

UPRIGHT: No.

Be careful what you wish for in a relationship. You may soon get what you want but there is a strong likelihood it will not satisfy you and may even leave you feeling defeated in some way. Sometimes the win is not worth the price you have to pay. You learn valuable lessons from surrender and defeat but the process will take its toll. It is a complicated situation with several people and maybe even family members involved. The time of defeat is the best time to sow the seeds of future successes. Communicate your needs. Don't act like you are a victim.

REVERSED: No.

You may get a variation on what you want and find that, in the end, it goes against your best interests. You may encounter defeat, either in your own situation or that of another. A hurtful secret could be discovered. Regrets about a love situation can cause you to blame yourself. A manipulative or mean-spirited person might be the problem. If someone's opinions are being overlooked and their needs disregarded, they will certainly feel like a victim. Be careful of thoughtlessness, harassment, or gossip. Even though someone is being very selfish, try to avoid blame and revenge.

SIX OF WINGS
PASSAGE

UPRIGHT: Yes!
You will make it! You have endured difficult times and your challenge now is to shake off what you've been through so you can make the most of the happy times that will soon come. You need to change your beliefs about yourself and realize that you are now in a much better position. You are more discerning and can make good decisions. Things are looking up. Give yourself permission to have fun. You have weathered the storm and should enjoy the moment. A trip will do you much good and may lead you to meet a person who will become very important to you.

REVERSED: Yes.
A trip may be delayed or disappoint. Cancellations create challenges. The improvement you hope to see in your relationship or search for true love may not come for a while. This test of patience will eventually be passed if you prepare now to endure and persevere. A more positive attitude, approach, or both are required, but someone is in a rut or doesn't want to work on unhealthy attitudes. What you believe about yourself and life in general also needs to change for the better. A calm and centered approach is the best way to get through the coming difficulties.

SEVEN OF WINGS
OPPOSITION

UPRIGHT: No!

The opposition you are encountering can work to your benefit. Be clever and observant in dealing with it or with destructive behavior or disappointing news. Evaluate the risk you are taking or encountering in relationships by staying rational and careful, even in the face of broken promises or difficult moods. Be logical, persistent, and use every trick you know without resorting to the immoral or the illegal. You may be tempted to stand someone up or be disheartened by an incorrect assumption. A wise counselor can help you see self-created problems and eliminate negative behavior patterns.

REVERSED: No.

Don't underestimate the formidable opposition you are encountering or creating. Even using every resource you have or can borrow to create or hold onto the relationship in question might not be enough, so make sure it is worth keeping. Negative behavior patterns must be overcome in yourself or another. Be aware of prejudice, fear, and deceit. Others involved may be evasive or misleading and refuse to state their true intentions. Untrustworthy people must be eliminated from your life. Try to correct mistakes as they occur. Don't go against your best interests.

EIGHT OF WINGS
INDECISION

UPRIGHT: Maybe.

If a decision regarding a potential partner or relationship must be made, gather as much information as you can but do not decide yet. In this case, the lack of a decision or even of clarity can somehow benefit you. Relax and contemplate the whole picture and what will bring you satisfaction and resolution. Rid yourself of outmoded beliefs about a particular person. In times of doubt and confusion be alert but do not act immediately. Pay attention to your gut instincts. Look patiently within for answers from your higher mind. No one else should decide for you.

REVERSED: No.

Being indecisive will work against you in this case. If you are feeling hopelessly alone or overly restricted by your relationship you will encounter a crisis of indecision in either yourself or another. One of you may not be able to commit to the relationship and are in it because of loneliness or resignation to circumstances. You may not be able to get yourself out of an unpleasant situation with a friend or lover because of family or the person's demands or disapproval. Decide not to be around toxic people or you will feel insecure and make inappropriate decisions.

NINE OF WINGS
OBSESSION

UPRIGHT: No!

Take time to confront and cope with an obsession, either yours or that of another person. Fixating on a particular outcome can derail a new or existing relationship by producing in you or your partner boring patterns of thinking, speaking, and acting. Thoughtlessness, cynicism, or an overly judgmental nature may also result. Disillusionment about true love, if not dealt with, can lead to compulsion, paranoia, or physical illness. Adequate sleep and meditation can reduce obsessing over endless doubts and fears. Professional counseling can help you act appropriately and heal.

REVERSED: No!

Fears and doubts must be confronted and understood or they will turn into compulsive behavior, paranoia, or physical illness. If obsession gets the better of you or a person overly interested in you, professional help may be required. Focusing on past mistakes is unhelpful. Unreasonable skepticism about finding true love may lead to depression. The difference between what your heart feels and what your head is telling you can be resolved if you stay productive. Wholeness can eventually be attained, but you may have to first make working on yourself your new obsession.

TEN OF WINGS
DIFFICULTY

UPRIGHT: No.

Though difficult times have come and may still be ongoing, the worst is over. You may be feeling completely drained. You have experienced a great deal of doubt and uncertainty in your relationships, a "dark night of the soul." It is especially hard to endure this alone. Sharing difficulties can strengthen a relationship. Problems faced together can produce the wisdom and compassion to help others in crisis. The hopes and dreams of the past may be dashed but new ones will arise in time. If words cannot comfort, a wound this deep and loss this devastating may require professional help.

REVERSED: No.

You may encounter or have already encountered a situation where the worst seems to have happened with an existing or potential lover. Tears shed may leave you feeling uncertain that true love can ever be yours. The hopes and dreams of the past may seem dashed. There may be remorse and anguish about a lost or broken relationship. Seek the support of others who have gone through similar difficulties. Feelings of hopelessness and/or being unloved and abandoned may indicate deep depression. Professional help is necessary to help you get yourself back on the path to true love.

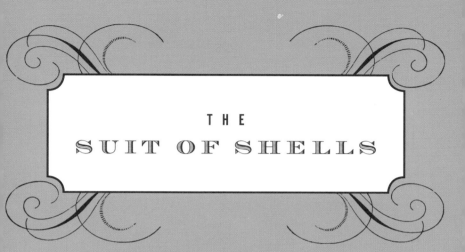

THE
SUIT OF SHELLS

PRINCESS OF SHELLS
THE ROMANTIC

UPRIGHT: Maybe.

The PRINCESS OF SHELLS upright is drying her hair after a dip in the ocean, symbol of humanity's collective unconscious. A male seahorse, the only species where the male gestates their young, has come to tell her the surprising news he is pregnant. The princess bursts into tears, feeling loving pride and the anticipation of future pain and suffering. She confides in her friend that she, too, longs to find a gentle, child-loving partner with whom to create a family.

You will encounter or find yourself acting like a young, sensitive, empathetic woman whose heart rules her head. Being an incurable romantic in love with love and always seeking a romantic encounter will benefit you now. You may feel inexperienced and not ready for the responsibilities that come with a serious relationship, but it is time to try. Communicate tender feelings, hunches, and dreams. Read or write romantic stories or poems. You are "pregnant" with romantic ideas and idealized fantasies and fertile in every way. Be careful if you don't want to have a child.

Psychic intuitions—yours and maybe that of an intuitive counselor—will enable you to navigate uncharted waters. This intuitive ability is always available to help you sort relationship problems—yours and your friends'. We continuously learn the lessons of love. You may be pleasantly surprised.

REVERSED: No.

The PRINCESS OF SHELLS reversed plays with her hair, afraid to go in the ocean because she doesn't like her appearance when she's wet, symbolizing she fears being overcome by emotions, intuitions, and psychic advice. A male seahorse shares the surprising news he is pregnant. The princess bursts into jealous tears, though the seahorse is her friend.

You will encounter or find yourself acting like an overly sensitive, intense young woman whose heart often gets her into confusing emotional conflicts. She is a sucker for a sob story and has a tendency to pick up stray animals and romantic partners. She is in denial of what her life's experiences have taught her and is terrified of the responsibilities that come along with a serious relationship. She has difficulty articulating her tender feelings, hunches, and dreams without feeling overwhelmed by them. Pregnancy should be addressed with care—now may not be the right time.

She can be jealous because she's disappointed she hasn't made her dreams of love come true. She's idealistic and gives her heart away too quickly. She loves the idea of love more than the reality. She worries about appearances, absorbed in the trends of the moment. A good person who is too soft or sensitive, she can be exploited and/or not taken seriously.

PRINCE OF SHELLS
THE CHARMER

UPRIGHT: Maybe.

The PRINCE OF SHELLS upright has his back to us, symbolizing he has rejected conventional notions of what is right and proper. His hunting horn hangs strangely limp in his hand, its bell turned toward the ground, signifying he doesn't want his ways or whereabouts known.

You are about to meet or explore taking on the qualities of a person like the PRINCE OF SHELLS. He may seem fey, strangely innocent, or merely flirtatious, but he is actually a Don Juan, skilled beyond his years in the ways of love. He acts boldly on his romantic, sensual, and sexual impulses and explores them in ways most people are too inhibited to even imagine. His bohemian lifestyle is attractive to those who romanticize its unrestricted, goal-less hedonism but even the prince will admit anything done to excess becomes boring.

Be charming to others, regardless of their sex, while still expressing a romantic, poetic view of life in your unique way. An extremely imaginative or provocative person—you or another—may introduce you to an exceptional, drama-loving circle. You may enjoy investigating alternative healing or spiritual teachings together. Your group's unusual interests will attract invitations and new contacts. Explore your sexuality carefully—you may be tempted to party with reckless abandon. Keep everything secret from those not ready to hear.

REVERSED: Maybe.

The PRINCE OF SHELLS is reversed and has his back to us, symbolizing he has not only rejected conventional notions of what is right and proper, he has turned notions of good and evil on their heads. His hunting horn touches the ground, signifying he wishes to elevate the most earthly pursuits to the heavens but has lost his sense of direction.

You are about to meet or confront the qualities within yourself of a person like the PRINCE OF SHELLS. He may seem to be a Don Juan, skilled beyond his years in the ways of love, who acts boldly on his romantic, sensual, and sexual impulses and explores them in ways most people are too inhibited to even imagine, but in actuality his appetites are out of control and a danger to himself and others.

His bohemian lifestyle is a façade—he is simply not capable of functioning successfully in the world and is floating through life. His excessive, goal-less hedonism now bores him and the misfits that pass for his friends. This could indicate an addictive personality. The need for more intense pleasures may deteriorate into empty promises and empty wine bottles.

Be careful with your sexuality and sexual practices. Someone may be lying to get you into bed. Another person is attracted to this someone and jealousy may erupt. You might discover someone close to you is a gigolo or, worse, a pervert.

QUEEN OF SHELLS
THE EMPATH

UPRIGHT: Maybe.

The eyes of The QUEEN OF SHELLS upright seem to look away from whomever she is talking to. Is she chooses to do so, however, she can "see" into a person's soul and future with her psychic intuition. She is a classically trained empath and can shield herself from the negativity of others. She cares deeply about all beings but is fully aware they each bear ultimate responsibility for what they do with what life has given them.

You are about to meet or be called upon to emulate a person with the compassion of the QUEEN OF SHELLS. It may be time to visit a reputable professional intuitive counselor. You and/or a romantic partner needs to be sympathetic to the foibles of human frailty, yours included. Be a shoulder to cry on, but offer advice only if it is specifically requested.

Be kind and compassionate, the truly spiritual way to live. Think with your heart, not your head. Learn how those in need cope with life's challenges. Share your knowledge of tolerance and humility. A sensitive, intuitive dreamer who acts on his or her dreams can teach you about affection, kindness, faith, and forgiveness. Articulating deep feelings may be hard, but there is a genuine ability to perceive people's inner emotions, maybe by channeling psychic information. Investigating astrology, the metaphysical, telepathic phenomena, and other ancient wisdom will bring true love into your life.

REVERSED: Maybe.

The eyes of the QUEEN OF SHELLS reversed look away because she cannot bear direct contact with others' reality—it is difficult for her to handle her own. She cannot control her psychic ability to "see" into a person's life, soul, and future and feels overwhelmed by her gift. She has not learned how to shield herself from others' negativity. She cares deeply and desires to "save" all beings from unpleasantness, but often ends up enabling their self-destructive actions.

You are about to meet or be called upon to see if you are a person with the confused ways of the QUEEN OF SHELLS reverse. You and/or a romantic partner need to stop being slaves to each other's bad habits or to intuitive guidance from questionable sources. You may meet or be someone who plays the victim, hoping he, she, or you will be rescued from guilt, spiritual pride, or egotism. Watch for co-dependent or enabling behavior in yourself or someone you love.

Adapt a harder shell so others won't take advantage of you. If you get too close, you may not be able to distinguish your feelings and needs from those of someone near you. Avoid people who are unreliable, wishy-washy, chronically late, or who have been unfaithful to you or another. Their neediness may become a burden or cause you heartbreak.

KING OF SHELLS
THE VISIONARY

UPRIGHT: Yes.

The KING OF SHELLS upright seems younger than his years. His creative, balanced, engaged approach to life and love have staved the ravages of age that afflict those less in harmony with the divine forces we see swirling around his head. He is a Renaissance man, inventor, accomplished artist, and well-read scholar. His gaze is direct and friendly but he is no fool. He is as sensitive and psychic as any in his family and uses this tool as one of many for enlightened rule of his kingdom. His psychic gifts are second nature to him. He is a true visionary who reads people and omens as well as he uses his creative powers to realize his visions. He is a counselor of counselors.

You will soon meet or be called upon to emulate the qualities of a person like the KING OF SHELLS upright. You need to understand why strong feelings have surfaced and how to cope with them. Do not repress your emotions. View your life as a work of art and your art as a work of life.

A time to experience a deep, long-lasting love and contentment approaches. Learn what gifts you have to give as a lover, parent, counselor, and friend. Give advice only to those you know are ready to hear it and to act on it. Study the teachings of a favorite spiritual master or philosopher. Visualize the true love you seek and you will realize it.

REVERSED: Maybe.

The KING OF SHELLS reversed is too young and self-centered to be a leader. He is creative and intuitive but is full of himself and—all too often—intoxicating substances, which cloud the way he presents himself. People are put off and/or confused by his unclear speech and imperious manner when he shares his visions. They don't know if it is his wealth, genetics, sexual proclivity, or the royal plastic surgeon's skill that have staved the ravages of age.

His gaze is direct, but his mind is somewhere else. He seems stuck in the past. He is as sensitive and psychic as any in his family but uses it to control people. He is a visionary whose psychic gifts burden him. He can read people and omens as skillfully as he uses his creative powers to realize his visions, though he is tired of being a counselor.

You will soon meet or be called upon to see if you display the haughty ways of a person like the KING OF SHELLS reversed. Strengths, gifts, and good fortune should not be lorded over others. Repressed emotions such as paranoia, insomnia, or panic attacks may crop up unexpectedly at inappropriate times.

It is all right not to get involved with others' problems—just don't upset them. You and/or your partner are high-strung and may be unable to forgive, accept love, or give advice now.

ACE OF SHELLS
LOVE

UPRIGHT: Yes!

You will soon experience the feeling of an exciting new romance. Your loving ways will magnetize love to you and there will be an ongoing relationship formed. Your heart will open and you will be moved emotionally. Unconditional love will be given and received in equal measure. An existing relationship will reach a new level. You will both be very attracted to each other. An existing relationship will see the deepening of your mutual emotional commitment. You are optimistic, full of happiness, and wellbeing. The realization of true love brings peace of mind and fills your heart with joy.

REVERSED: Yes.

You want to encounter or feel the heady excitement and promise of new love, even in an existing relationship, but fear of commitment in you or another person may make you feel vaguely unfulfilled. You may have been deeply hurt by a parent, lover, or even a thoughtless friend. You could be in for a new and unpleasant surprise in the form of the childish behavior of an ego-driven person. You or your love interest might not be able to open your hearts to love now because of old wounds. You need help to get past this inhibition, as you may harbor unconscious shame that must be examined and healed.

TWO OF SHELLS
ROMANCE

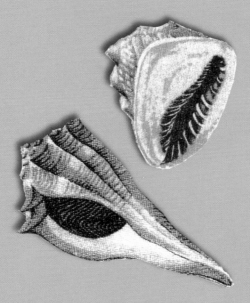

UPRIGHT: Yes!

Two hearts can beat as one. If you are alone, it is time to turn on your "'love light"—your willingness to listen, share, and commit yourself with all your heart will pay off. True love is coming to you soon. Alone or with someone, you will soon get the rare chance to know the clear, nurturing, supportive, and heart-felt emotional exchange that is the mark of a good romantic relationship. Few things are more valuable. Your passionate feelings will be reciprocated. There is an easy, pleasurable attraction and compatibility, with great conversation and, if the time is right, enjoyable sex.

REVERSED: Yes.

You seem to be close to having the nurturing, supportive, and heartfelt exchange of emotions that is the gift of a romantic relationship. Be sure you're not lost in daydreams and fantasies about a relationship that isn't real. Even if love seems to have found you, doubt and indecision haunt. You may like your independence and are resistant to making the accommodations that true love requires. You may be attracted to someone but cannot let him or her or the world know. Give your relationship time and breathing room to develop. Push too hard or too fast and true love may fade away.

THREE OF SHELLS
CELEBRATION

UPRIGHT: Yes, have fun!

It's party time! Don't be alone no matter how important your work seems. Enjoying yourself is as important as working hard. Opportunities abound for wonderfully romantic days and nights, so take advantage of them. Put your worries aside and feel gratitude for life's gifts. If you're looking for love or are in a relationship, go on a trip or attend a celebration. Just make sure that happy people surround you with good wishes. Speak your heart about whom and what is important to you. Do what makes you happy. This is a time to give thanks and enjoy the best life has to offer.

REVERSED: Yes.

Expectations for a celebration or vacation may not be realized. Someone might cancel or behave poorly. Your search for true love can prove difficult because too many or too few opportunities to celebrate exist. A love relationship needs to be grounded in reality. The two of you have to be compatible when the party's over. If you have no reasons or opportunities to celebrate, make up some reasons and write "celebrate" on your "To Do" list. All work and no play will make anyone a dull and lonely person. This card reversed can also be a warning not to overindulge.

FOUR OF SHELLS
RE-EVALUATION

UPRIGHT: Maybe.

It is time to re-evaluate a relationship or someone's attitude about relationships in general. Old feelings may no longer be valid or valued. A fresh start may be needed. If you are bored or dissatisfied with the status quo, avoid distractions and examine your heart of hearts to gain clarity. How you feel is most important now. If you are feeling shy, tired, or bogged down, you need to take time for introspection to break out of old, unproductive patterns. Forgiving each other and setting new goals will sooth harsh or stress-producing communications between you and your partner.

REVERSED: No.

Either too much or too little re-evaluation can be detrimental to your search for true love now. Try to appear consistent to someone you're interested in. Constantly playing "s/he loves me, s/he loves me not" or "I love him/her, I love him not" is going to work against you. Avoid "crying over spilt milk" or saying "I told you so." It is not attractive, and complaining will only inflame the problem. On the other hand, someone in the relationship may be ignoring major changes that have taken place. Whether these changes are for better or worse, they must be acknowledged and acted upon.

FIVE OF SHELLS
DISAPPOINTMENT

UPRIGHT: No.

You may feel left behind or have to leave someone else behind, but it is all for the best. You need to understand rejection, disappointment, and indifference. Realize the ways your disappointment gains you experience that can help ensure future success. Try looking at the glass as half full instead of half empty. Learn about the mind-body connection. Examine how your thoughts have affected this difficult situation. You may be carrying old baggage from a former relationship that is preventing you from sorting out your mixed feelings and making honest choices about a new person.

REVERSED: No!

Past disappointments may be preventing you from enjoying the present. A period of disappointment, indifference, or rejection can cause confusion as to how to react. Walking away from the relationship may not solve the underlying problem. Problems that are not severe can often be dealt with in the relationship or they will only come back again in a different form or a different relationship. Staying with someone you should leave because of violence or other forms of abuse can have devastating effects, especially if children are involved. Professional help might be necessary.

SIX OF SHELLS
JOY

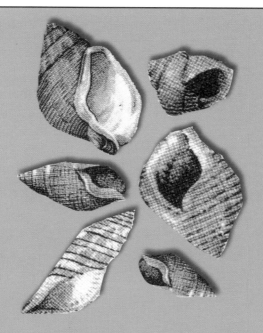

UPRIGHT: Yes!
Child-like joy will soon be yours and maybe even an actual child, if that's what you've asked about. You can benefit from time spent with younger people. Your beliefs about bringing children into a relationship will be respected. Remember nostalgic memories of childhood friends and family. Lighten up. Make time for fun. Be as open and optimistic as a child. You may meet someone with a similar upbringing or background. Someone you used to know or love could come back into your life. You can find true love if you display the wisdom of years and the innocence of youth.

REVERSED: Yes.
Children, childish behavior, or conflicting attitudes about bringing children into a relationship may be preventing you from finding true love. A triggered nostalgic memory of childhood can cause difficulties. Dwelling on the past or on a loss of friendship or innocence is counterproductive. A child, someone raised the way you were, or someone from your past may appear in your life now but it may cause you heartache. You or the person you care about may have anxiety about what lies ahead. You are not taking enough time to just have fun. You need to balance work with play.

SEVEN OF SHELLS
ILLUSION

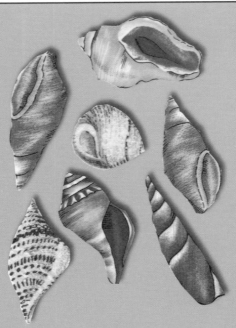

UPRIGHT: Maybe.

You can go out with a lot of different people but don't give your heart to anyone until s/he clearly distinguishes him or herself as "the one." Separate what is real from what is an illusion. Are you idolizing someone or are they having unrealistic expectations about you? Protect against unclear or wishful thinking or you'll be riding an emotional rollercoaster of big mood swings about your love life. Your vivid imagination can help you manifest true love if your intentions are clear. See a picture of what you want in your mind's eye and know that you can create it because you deserve it.

REVERSED: No.

Going out with a lot of people causes problems. You will encounter illusion, confusion, or distraction. It may be hard to focus your energies now. Avoid intoxication and other forms of escapism in yourself and/or others. A suspected deception may be confirmed. Wishful thinking can lead to an unrealistic pursuit or infatuation. Distinguish creative inspiration from pipedreams. Idealism often leads to disillusionment. You or someone you know may be misinterpreting ambiguous intentions. Postpone decisions until you are sure what is best to do. Be realistic. Avoid living in a fantasy world.

EIGHT OF SHELLS
SACRIFICE

UPRIGHT: No.

You need to be more aware of the physical, mental, or emotional sacrifices that are or will become required regarding what you have asked about. It could be worth it but you may need to seek a person or cause more worthy of your efforts and sacrifice. Work on your tendency towards shyness and withdrawal by not taking yourself so seriously. You or someone you love may swing from sudden outbursts of crying to emotional frigidity and back again. It may seem that you are going through a dark night of the soul, but you are actually learning about self-love and self-nurturing.

REVERSED: No!

There needs to be more awareness of the physical, mental, or emotional sacrifices that are involved in what you have asked about. It is a precarious time, infused with doubt and pessimistic thoughts. Even a dream relationship can turn into a nightmare if there is an imbalance of sacrifice. True love requires sacrifice from both partners. Letting go or moving on is scary but if you are continually giving more than you are getting, you need to find a more worthy partner or cause. Don't be surprised if true love eludes you if you are the one who is refusing to sacrifice in equal measure.

NINE OF SHELLS
FULFILLMENT

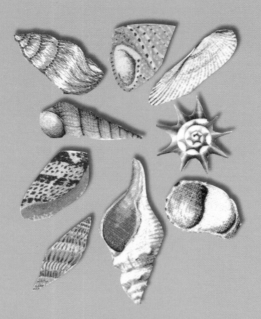

UPRIGHT: Yes!

You will find true love as if by magic. Your wish will be granted in a happy way. When formulating your wish be sure to phrase it as precisely as you possibly can. The process of deciding what wish you would like to see granted can help you understand your desires and priorities. Be aware that your wish may be granted in an unexpected manner. Now is the time for success, good health, and a wonderful partnership. You will come to know what fulfillment in a relationship really is. Your relationship will create your own enchanted world and the realization of your deepest desires.

REVERSED: Yes.

A wish will be granted but in a way that really doesn't satisfy or actually causes more annoyance than pleasure. Be careful what you wish for and how you wish for it. You and/or a love interest may fear your luck has run out and that you can never get what you want. This can be a difficult time if you're too used to getting your way. Incompatible opinions about finances or possessiveness might also create problems. Someone may try to "buy" your favor or try to sabotage your attempts to make positive changes. Arrogance about an important decision can work against your relationship.

TEN OF SHELLS
SUCCESS

UPRIGHT: Yes!
Congratulations! You have succeeded in becoming who you need to be for true love to enter your life and relationship. If you are involved with a new love, it is the real thing. In fact, this card may indicate a wedding. Be more aware of how successful and respected you are. You will never enjoy your success until you empower yourself by appreciating what you have done. You will have a safe and secure situation at home. There is a feeling of wholeness and stability. This time of contentment in your relationship will inspire peaceful and loving interactions between you and all those you care about.

REVERSED: Yes.
You are very close to being whom you need to be to bring true love into your life and/or relationships but you may not see or believe it. Pessimism can stop you from making your success real. Someone you care about may not be feeling successful and/or respected. A reward or goal that was expected may be diminished or delayed. Interference from friends or relatives or both can complicate things. Worrying about or trying to "fix" frustrating and dysfunctional family interactions can waste time and energy. A manipulative or unstable person may affect your reputation.

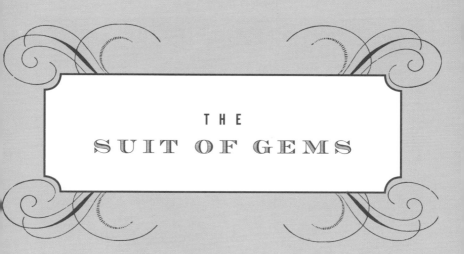

THE
SUIT OF GEMS

PRINCESS OF GEMS
THE INGÉNUE

UPRIGHT: Yes.

The PRINCESS OF GEMS upright prepares to play a flute she has made in a garden she has planted. Many city dwellers in her kingdom think she is naïve and unsophisticated, but those who know that we all live off the land see her clearly as being one with the world that gives her life. She's not afraid of getting her hands dirty or of any honest work. She loves and communicates with the plants and animals and the spirit in all things, even gems and rocks. She is wealthy because she knows how to live off the land and how to get what she wants. She is sensuality personified.

You will soon encounter or explore in your own life the qualities of a person like the PRINCESS OF GEMS. Be practical, persevere, and trust your natural instincts—don't be afraid of seeming naïve or unsophisticated.

A new partner will be down-to-earth, good with his or her hands, and/or able to create wealth in some way. The communication of practical information and/or useful skills will aid you in your search for true love.

A new business idea could evolve. That process will create loyal and supportive relationships. Your work or career is very important now. A hands-on person who is connected with your business interests may become your new love interest. You may work together for money, charity, or on hobbies and crafts such as a home renovation. Gardening, pets, or classes may also improve your love life in many ways.

REVERSED: Maybe.

The PRINCESS OF GEMS reversed enjoys all the benefits of her parents' wealth but takes her good fortune for granted. She has no idea how to support herself or how those less fortunate live. Even when she tries to act worldly, those with real-life experience see she is naïve, unsophisticated, and lacking in common sense and awareness of human nature. She's afraid of working or getting dirty, though she is willing to do dirty deeds to protect her lifestyle. She sees everyone and everything as toys to play with then discard at will. She is anxious because at her core she knows how dependent on others and fortunate circumstances she is. She seeks pleasure but has trouble letting go and surrendering to love.

You will soon encounter or rid yourself of the qualities of a person like the PRINCESS OF GEMS. You and or/your partner may have difficulty being practical. You may give up too easily. Don't fear being thought of as naïve or unsophisticated. If you need something explained, ask.

A new or existing partner may be unkempt, uncouth or antagonistic to your way of enjoying life. This person may try to force you to change your ways, your job, or your finances.

Seek practical information and/or useful skills or your career will suffer. Someone quite younger than you and/or in an inferior position to you at work may become your new love interest.

PRINCE OF GEMS
THE BUILDER

UPRIGHT: Yes.

The shield, axe, and staff the PRINCE OF GEMS upright holds symbolize he is a responsible, trustworthy, and respected member of his kingdom's construction, support, and defense forces. He knows nothing is free, especially the freedom he and his fellow citizens enjoy, and must be built with a strong foundation. He is ambitious and has risen in rank on his own merits. His nakedness symbolizes his purity, health, and self-confidence. He is strong in every way and his earthy sense of humor hides a seriousness born from seeing firsthand the realities of life and death.

You will soon either meet or be called upon to display the qualities of a person like the PRINCE OF GEMS upright. This person may be physically strong, assertive, and goal-oriented, and/or skilled in politics and/or organizational dynamics. Your meeting will take place while you or he or she are either working or otherwise taking care of business, possibly the realization of a lucrative new business idea.

Honest hard work, property investment, and accumulating a nest egg are important now. Patience is required. Expect perseverance, sanity, common sense, and groundedness but not an impulsive, "hot" affair with this slow but steady person. It will take time for the heart of this reliable, good provider to open. Value true love above gain and possessions. Enjoying earthly delights together will bond and rejuvenate you before you get back to work.

REVERSED: Maybe.

The shield, axe, and staff held by naked PRINCE OF GEMS reversed symbolize he feels vulnerable and by clinging to material objects he can protect himself from the harsh world. He strives to be a responsible, trustworthy, and respected member of his kingdom's construction, support, and defense forces for his father's sake, but his own heart just isn't in it. He would prefer to inherit the kingdom because he is the prince rather than work for it. He can put the finishing touches on things, but he knows little about the importance of building from the ground up on a strong foundation. He is ruthlessly ambitious and has risen in the ranks by questionable means. He uses his considerable strength and skills, not to serve and protect, but to further his interests. His sophomoric gallows humor helps him push away the terrifying realities of life and death.

You will soon either meet or be called upon to see if you display the qualities of a person like the PRINCE OF GEMS reversed. This person may be skilled in political gamesmanship. Your may meet while you and/or he or she are either working or otherwise taking care of business.

Work, property investment, and accumulating a nest egg are so important to this person that true love may be beyond his or her power to give or receive. Do not let this person control you or your finances—you will lose out. If someone is cheap with money, they are usually cheap with love too.

QUEEN OF GEMS
THE NURTURER

UPRIGHT: Yes.

The smoldering gaze of the QUEEN OF GEMS upright reveals she is the most sensual of the tarot's royalty. She has found true love with her husband and loves nurturing her children in their supportive, well-functioning family. She is a born aristocrat and learned as a child that great wealth brings great responsibility. She is charitable and a patron and an astute collector of art, fashion, and jewelry and all things of value, especially knowledge. She makes sure her kingdom's schools and libraries are as full and up-to-date as her many closets.

You will soon meet or be called upon to emulate the qualities of the QUEEN OF GEMS. Now is the time to manifest your true love dreams. Appreciate and protect your good fortune and that of those you care about. Share your feelings in a straightforward way, taking charge while being receptive to other's needs.

Charitable events can provide you with social connections that greatly benefit you and introduce you to thoughtful and successful people. Socializing can connect you to people and situations that help foster love. Patronize the arts, go shopping, and/or enjoy your wealth as best you can, as long as you save for a rainy day.

Take or teach a class in cooking, baking, or even lovemaking! Live life to the full. Appreciate the gifts of beauty and grace all around you. Prepare to experience a true soul-mate connection. It is time to be enchanted!

REVERSED: Maybe.

The haughty gaze of the QUEEN OF GEMS reversed reveals she thinks she's better than everyone and her wish is your command. She takes for granted her good fortune and the true love her husband displays for her. She can't be bothered nurturing her children and foists them off on nannies and relatives. She is an aristocratic snob, and judges people by their lineage, wealth, and profession. She does her charitable work to keep up appearances. She would rather shop and spend money with abandon. She respects education as yet another badge of rank with which to judge people.

You will soon meet or be called upon to see if you display the qualities of the QUEEN OF GEMS. You can manifest true love if you stop judging people by what they have and start appreciating them for who they are inside.

You may be protecting your privacy to the point of being emotionally cold and insensitive. Patronizing the arts and working for charities can provide you with social connections, but people you encounter may disappoint you. Build a better relationship with a partner and/or your children.

You can protect your good fortune and that of those you care about too. A person who is important to you may be unable to help you now. Overspending or financial matters can negatively affect the status of a relationship. Take a class in cooking, baking, or even lovemaking!

KING OF GEMS
THE REALIST

UPRIGHT: Yes.

The KING OF GEMS upright leans on his staff, symbolizing it has been a long, hard climb to achieve his wealth, success, and power. He realizes he didn't do it without help. He has great respect and appreciation for those who work for him and prefers their company to that of the nobles crowding his court, making requests of him. He handles them and his many businesses well because he is mature and pragmatic. He is a realist with an earthy sense of humor and has experienced life from all sides. He loves his queen with all his heart and soul and puts their relationship first, ahead of everyone and everything, even his children.

You will soon meet or be required to display the qualities of a person like the KING OF GEMS. You will find a charismatic partner who loves you just as you are. You and/or your partner will reach a position of power and/or will be respected by those you respect.

Accept meeting and lunch invitations, and make dating, mating, and relating a priority. Interact with everyone, no matter what their status. Be yourself but put others at ease by respecting their origins.

Get down to basics in your relationship. Keep it simple. Massage each other. Seek outdoor activities and athletic types. Be natural, realistic, and committed. A sensible, pragmatic, serious-minded individual will appear in your life. A down-to-earth relationship will endure.

REVERSED: Maybe.

The KING OF GEMS reversed leans on his staff to symbolize he has retired from a life of pomp, responsibility, and ceremony. He has renounced his wealth and position to embark on a journey to find the meaning of life. He is determined to walk the great philosophers of the ages' path, learning from everyone he encounters, respecting their attempts to make sense of their lives. His earthy sense of humor is touched with a hint of sorrow because he is a realist and has compassion for those less fortunate. He loves his queen with all his heart and soul but no longer puts their relationship first.

You will soon meet or be required to examine your attitude toward the qualities of a person like the KING OF GEMS. You may find true love when you retire or with someone who is retired. Retirement may improve an existing relationship.

You will improve your relationship by studying ultimate truths. You may find a charismatic partner who loves you just as you are, but he or she may love everyone equally and is not interested in settling down. He or she may have attitudes, habits, and quirks that make being together difficult. Survival issues can cause this person to shun modern ways and the trappings of civilization. A misguided search for what is real may lead him or her to have unreal expectations or outright disdain for what a monogamous, true love relationship can be.

ACE OF GEMS
REWARD

UPRIGHT: Yes!

You will soon be rewarded. You will finally attain and make the most of what you have hoped, planned, and worked for. It is most likely a greatly improved love life, but you may also win something giving you more wealth, power, and/or status. It may come to you as the realization of a dream, gift, inheritance, bonus, promotion, or other reward. Sex appeal, new adventures, and good chemistry between you and a partner who loves you are indicated. Good news regarding children and animals is also indicated. Savor this time and realize that you have earned it whether you or anyone else thinks you have.

REVERSED: Yes.

You will soon be rewarded with a new opportunity to attain a dream—make the most of it! If you sit back and expect things to come to you, you might lose out on a great relationship or miss receiving a reward, bonus, or inheritance. Receiving a reward has its problems. More money brings more responsibilities and temptations. Others will want or even expect things from you. Weight gain or lack of purpose can be a turn-off. Avoid using money to manipulate others or you will be manipulated. Without mutual interests, even the most passionate lovers can become self-absorbed and disagreeable.

TWO OF GEMS
CHANGE

UPRIGHT: Maybe.
You or someone you love must cope with constant change and/or busyness. Stay centered and flexible. Keep yourself informed. Allow yourself to be who-ever you want to be with whomever you are with. Now is a time you may want to keep two or more relationships going rather than focus on just one. Keep your options open while you take the time to figure out how you really feel. Stay busy and involved in a variety of activities. The issue you must focus on now is how to best juggle relationships, career, and family. You might meet someone special under extraordinary circumstances!

REVERSED: Maybe.
You may be tested by a period of incredible busyness, change, and instability. The hectic pace will make you or a loved one irritable and nervous. Focusing on two or more things at once—especially two or more relationships—could cause problems now. Trying to stay flexible is draining when you are pulled in too many directions. You may not be able to keep everything going and have to pick up the pieces and start again. Problems might be caused by a changeable person or someone who is two-faced or hiding their problems from you, the world, and maybe even from him or herself—make sure it's not you.

THREE OF GEMS
WORK

UPRIGHT: Yes.

Romance or love may come to you through your work or your career efforts, which are also blessed by this card. Accept invitations that are supportive of your career or other ambitions. In an existing relationship you and your partner will equitably share the work of establishing or maintaining it. This mutual support will enable you to grow it further. It is a good time to seek the advice of a trusted friend or counselor and/or to share techniques, solutions, and business aspirations with a partner. You may end up working with the person you love, possibly in your own business.

REVERSED: Yes.

It takes two committed people to make a relationship work. If you don't have that now, remember you don't need another person to complete you. You are complete even when you are alone. Maintaining that attitude will help you find true love. Use caution regarding a relationship that comes to you through your work or career efforts. Be careful about getting involved romantically with a superior, co-worker, or even some kind of service worker. Avoid triangulating your relationships. Children need to know that you are happy and secure in your relationship. If you are not, do something about it.

FOUR OF GEMS
POSSESSIVENESS

UPRIGHT: Maybe.

You need to hold on to what you have. You're better off being single than wasting your time and throwing away the precious gift of love. If you're in a relationship, it's natural to be a little jealous now and then. It's a sign that you value your partner, and it can also increase passion. Take care of your home and family. It is time to think like a successful executive. What you save and conserve now will greatly benefit you in the future. Build a strong foundation, take responsibility, and keep your eye on the prize and your affairs in order. Manage your possessions well and guard them carefully.

REVERSED: Maybe.

Loss is possible now even if you hold onto what you have. You or another may be overly possessive or trying to recapture what is clearly gone, when letting go might be the better course of action. Only a relationship that fosters spiritual growth and reflects your true values should be retained and protected. If you have that, fight for it. Don't treat people like objects—no one belongs to anyone else, even if they love each other. Physical possessions cannot satisfy a longing for true love. Save for a rainy day, but don't hoard. Those who are cheap with their resources are stingy with their love too.

FIVE OF GEMS
ANXIETY

UPRIGHT: No.

You might feel left out of "the party." You need to learn to cope with stress and anxiety if you are to find true love or improve an existing relationship. Developing the ability to balance logic and intuition is vital now. Don't waste time worrying about what happened years ago or what might happen in the future. Obsessive thoughts can stop you from living well. Too much focus on problems and not solutions can drain your energy. Take little steps to go forward, even in the face of fear. Panic attacks are disorders that have a cause and can be cured by cognitive therapy or with professional help.

REVERSED: No.

You may have to cope with stress, anxiety, or denial. You might feel a lack of respect, support, or understanding. Distance or separation can cause despair. You and/or your partner could be worrying too much about things you can't change and/or not enough about things you can. Worry can paralyze you or make you act inappropriately until you face its source. Focus on the present and do what you can with what you have. Actual panic disorder is a disease. Professional guidance can help you heal any frightening, conflicting feelings and emotional upheavals that are threatening you and your relationship.

SIX OF GEMS
GENEROSITY

UPRIGHT: Yes!

Kindness and generosity are indicated. The good you have done will soon come back to you in many ways, including through the actions of a wonderful partner. You and your partner will be there for each other and in agreement about financial matters and goals. There will be the kind of mutual sharing of all things that is the mark of true love. If you are able, continue to give to those less fortunate. If you are in need, ask and it will be given to you. Look on the light and bright side of life. Be thankful for everything you have and count your blessings if you have good health and love.

REVERSED: Yes.

It may seem like the generosity you have shown is not being reciprocated. There can be a conflict in the value systems of you and a love interest. You or the other person might not be able to meet each other's expectations and financial needs. The other person might be selfish and be unable to share. You may not receive what you ask for, and that lack of sensitivity can hurt your feelings. The person may be jealous of what you have because he or she has unfulfilled dreams. The repayment of a debt or gift might be delayed. A petty, cheap, or needy person may annoy you.

SEVEN OF GEMS
FRUSTRATION

UPRIGHT: No.

To find true love you must deal with frustration. If things aren't going as planned, remember that almost all expectations are unreasonable—there are no guarantees. There may be potential for growth in a relationship but there is the need to cope with a frustrating person—make sure that person isn't you! Saving for retirement, a home, a vehicle, or an education are all smart things to do, but budgetary restrictions always cause frustration. It is noble to do what you can with what you have. Count your blessings. Seek attainable goals. Spend quality time together. Take time to laugh, caress, and play.

REVERSED: No.

More hard work is needed before you see results. Frustration may get the better of you when you try to cope with feelings of impotence and ingratitude in a relationship. You may think you can't accomplish enough with the resources you have. Confusion about responsibilities can cause problems. Promises may get broken. Money or work problems can put true love on hold for a while. Someone may have double standards—he or she can dish it out but can't take it. Be careful not to rush into an affair. A frustrating person you care about may get into an impractical or unrealistic romance.

EIGHT OF GEMS
PERFECTIONISM

UPRIGHT: Yes.

Romantic endeavors and other contests will be successful. You will master the art of love and make wise choices and practical efforts that will contribute to the success of a partnership. You know how to make your loved ones feel special. Working steadily towards your vision will bring deep satisfaction. A relationship may form as the result of your creative interests. You are wise to approach your relationship like a skilled craftsperson: do not think about results or rewards, study your subject, learn as you work, attend to all details with love and skill, and avoid perfectionism.

REVERSED: Yes.

You will create a great relationship or improve an existing one if you can focus solely on the task at hand and avoid perfectionism. You may find true love, win an award, or otherwise be recognized for your abilities but not if you focus on the end result and don't take things a step at a time. An imbalance of resources, status, or achievement might present problems in your relationship. If someone is overly critical, withholds praise, or lets fear, mistrust, and control stand in the way of true love, then it is time for a more perfect relationship.

NINE OF GEMS
INDEPENDENCE

UPRIGHT: Yes!

Your love life will soon improve dramatically if you work on becoming or simply appearing independent, free, and self-reliant. Get out into the natural world and enjoy pleasant outdoor activities with a loved one. If you're looking for love, you may find it outdoors. Learn about your body and how Mother Nature provides all that is needed. Treat your health as your greatest wealth. Emphasize your best physical attributes. Develop a strong sense of yourself. You will achieve success if you stick to your plan. You have accomplished a lot—it is time to harvest the fruits of your labors.

REVERSED: Yes.

Independence is an important issue now. You or your love interest may be too independent. A person enjoying true love feels freer than ever in a relationship. True love means wanting your partner to feel safe and secure enough to be fully him or herself. If you and/or your partner believe you are not as independent, free, and self-reliant as you need to be, there must be beliefs, values, and priorities that go against what is required by true love. Let Nature be your guide. Take care of your health. Get out in the country. Too much time at home may make your waistline increase.

TEN OF GEMS
PROTECTION

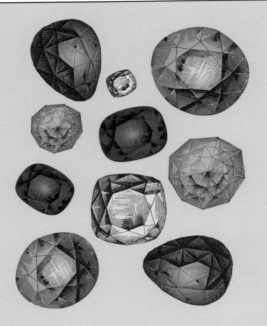

UPRIGHT: Yes!

True love is destined to be yours—sooner rather than later. A relationship that has been built securely from the ground up will survive the test of time. Past ties and rich family traditions offer support and protection. An important holiday or other celebration can lead to new prospects for love. Seeds you planted in the past bear fruit now. It is a good time to make important decisions. Living together is so strongly favored that there may soon be a wedding planned. You may establish your own dynasty. Your success is assured if you invest conservatively and do not gamble.

REVERSED: Yes!

You are close to finding true love, but security issues must first be resolved. You and/or your partner may feel either extremely vulnerable and unprotected or smothered by each other and/or by established rules and structures. The realities surrounding wealth, status, and influence can become burdensome obstacles if you don't have true love's spirit of kindness, understanding, and compromise to guide you. One or both of you might be too worried about what other people do or say, especially your relatives. An inheritance may be delayed or disappointing. A prenuptial agreement can cause problems.

SPELLS

FOR

TRUE LOVE

SPELLS, RITUALS, AND ENCHANTMENTS can help us remember that we are part of the rhythms and cycles of nature. Today the popular conception of the word ritual has come to conjure up images of indigenous (native) peoples spending their time and resources performing quaint, albeit beautiful, ceremonies that do not seem to benefit them. Others may think of rituals as the dry litany of words recited by rote in houses of worship. Like so many other aspects of modern life, ritual does not so much need a new definition as it needs to recapture the essence of its original meaning.

The indigenous peoples are not wasting their time when performing traditional ceremonies—they are reaffirming their connection to the natural world. The litany we hear in our houses of worship was originally designed to reaffirm faith and to awaken participants' religious experience.

The various offerings, prayers, affirmations, songs, stories, and any other ritual techniques that were employed before the occurrence of fortunate events were duly noted and used again and again.

One of the primary functions of ritual is to build a spiritual connection in our daily lives. Spells and rituals acknowledge the existence of a higher power, in ourselves and in our world. They also reinforce our desires and strengthen our intent as we work to materialize those desires.

Always perform the spells in a safe manner. Be careful when using candles and incense. Never leave a candle or any flame burning unattended. All fires should be made in well ventilated areas and in appropriately strong and fireproof metal or ceramic containers that are stable and have walls to prevent sparks from leaping out. Exercise caution using scissors and any sharp objects.

FOR ATTRACTING LOVE

Prepare an altar and decorate it with symbols of love that inspire you: photos of beautiful things, scents, and bits and pieces of colored fabrics.

Prepare a white candle by inscribing with a pencil point the words: "My true love comes to me."

Place the white candle in a secure holder in the center of the altar. Light it. Sit comfortably and gaze upon the flame while you visualize your love coming to you in harmony and beauty. As the candle burns down, collect the wax puddle that remains, wrap it up with some fabric from the altar, and keep it in a safe place.

FOR SELF-EMPOWERMENT

~

As you take a shower or bath, meditate upon your intention for self-empowerment. Allow yourself to feel your beauty and inner strength. Let go of the critic's voice for which you have no need. Visualize all the negativity you carry with you washing away, down the drain.

After you are finished, when you dry yourself off, look into a mirror and imagine a glowing white light all around you. Say the following words to yourself:

I feel my beauty,
And my inner strength.
I will allow my love, light,
And laughter to empower me,
And those around me.

FOR COMMUNICATING LOVE

~

Write the person you are interested in a sincere letter. Sprinkle the paper with a beautiful perfume, then draw your fingernails down the paper in wavy "snake lines" to mark it. Write their name on an envelope and put the letter inside.

Next, hold the letter to your heart and formulate your specific desire in your mind's eye. Focus your inner will upon achieving the result you wish to accomplish. Accept that as you asked, so shall it be done. Place the letter under your pillow for three nights, then burn it or bury it in a safe place.

TO BE OPEN TO RECEIVE LOVE

~

Find a fresh pink rose and put it in a vase with water. Take a pink candle and mark three hearts on it for your body, mind, and spirit.

Place it in a holder, and light it. Say:

I pray to receive,
A love who is true.
Open the door,
That I may meet,
Someone new.

FOR RELIEVING STRESS

~

Pick a small bunch of petals off some white flowers. Fill a beautiful bowl half full with water. Sprinkle the petals on the water as you say:

Truth and beauty,
Blessed be.
Remove from this water,
All hostility.
Flowers of love,
Blessed be,
Bring to my mind,
Peace and tranquility.

Allow the petals to float freely on the surface of the water. Put the bowl in front of you and allow your thoughts to float as lightly as the petals. Imagine the water being charged with positive energy from the beauty of the flowers and the love of the universe.

TO END A FIGHT

~

Find a quartz crystal. Place it before you, along with a glass of water. Allow yourself to relax and feel peaceful. When you are relaxed, think about the quarrel and say:

The time is now,
For this fight to end.
Let hurt be healed,
Begin the mend.

Repeat this until you can feel much of the hurt about the argument floating away. Wash off the quartz crystal. Pour the water down the drain. If you feel yourself getting angry repeat the spell.

TO BRING BACK A LOST LOVE

~

Place two pink candles on your altar, along with a photo of your lost love. Light the candles. Chant the following two times:

Universe of love,
Hear my prayer!
Bring passion and fire,
Hear my desire.
If it is meant to be,
Bring my true love back to me.

FOR OPENING YOUR
HEART CHAKRA

~

Lie down, relax, and get comfortable. Close your eyes.

Send your attention to the area of your heart chakra located in the middle of your chest. In your mind see a white light turn into a swirling vortex of green energy spinning clock-wise in the area of your chest. Feel the cleansing energy flow through your heart.

Breathe in and out slowly as you see the green whirling light clear out any blocks you may have.

Imagine breathing in Love…Compassion…Trust.

Imagine breathing out Self-pity…Paranoia…Sadness. See these worries diappearing into the whirling green vortex of energy.

You are forgiving. You are peaceful. You are a healer. Experience the love, light, and laughter that fills your heart with the joy of intimacy.

Now see the green color turn back into a white light that spreads throughout your body. Continue to relax.

Let out a deep sigh. AAHHHHH. Open your eyes.

TO BECOME MORE POSITIVE

~

Take an orange candle and some citrus oil. Find a quiet time and place, away from all distractions. Place the candle on the altar with the oil. Now engrave the candle with your name, using a pen point. While you anoint the candle with the oil, speak these words out loud or silently to yourself:

I clear my thoughts with the light of the sun.
Let my positive spell be done.
Candle burn to strengthen my will.
This spell be cast, for good, not ill.

Light the candle and place it in a safe place so it can burn down completely.

TO OVERCOME LONELINESS

~

Take a piece of paper and a pen and focus on your loneliness. With this feeling, write on the piece of paper:

Loneliness, please let me be.
Let me flee from your misery.
I pray for comfort, warmth, and friends,
Who truly love me for who I am.

Fold up the piece of paper and imagine the loneliness being locked inside. Bury it in the earth or throw it out with the garbage.

TO RECOVER FROM A
BROKEN HEART

~

Loosely bind a feather with a thin thread to a tree and say the following:

Heartache, please release me.
Despair, please leave me.
Wind and feather, please free me. Walk away. When the wind tugs the feather
from the tree, you will be freed.

TO DREAM OF LOVE

~

Write your wish on a piece of paper. Fold the paper in half, then half again. Draw an open eye inside of a heart on the outside of the folded page. Place the folded paper under your pillow and before bed repeat as follows:

With an open heart I seek to see,
What my future holds for me.
Be it good or be it ill,
Reveal my wish—that is my will.

Upon awakening, let your mind's eye capture the message your dream held for you. Let the dream symbols speak to you.

TO END OBSESSIVE FEELINGS

~

Focus your thoughts on the person over whom you no longer want to obsess. Think of all the reasons you need to let go of these feelings. Write the name of the person on a small slip of paper. Cross out the name with deliberation while you say to yourself:

You no longer have a place,
Within my heart—you are not my taste.
I will bury my feelings for you,
And then I can begin anew.

Bury this bit of paper and all your feelings about the person outside under a new moon.

TO OVERCOME JEALOUSY

~

Think of the person you are jealous of or the person who is jealous of you. Write the person's name on a piece of paper. Write these words on the other side:

Mother Nature, fair and true,
This emotion I offer unto you.
Heal the negative feelings within,
And help me to release and win!

Fold the paper, with the name inside. Place the folded paper against your forehead. Pass your right hand over it three times, mentally getting rid of all bad feelings. Put it in your freezer for a month then throw it away.

FOR STARTING OVER

~

Just before sunrise, go outside with a stick of incense. Face east, light the incense, and welcome the feeling of starting anew. Say:

With this beginning,
With this dawn of day,
I welcome the start,
Of a creative new way!

Watch as the wind carries away the smoke from the incense. Watch the sun rise and feel its rays cleansing you for the new day ahead.

TO MAKE LOVE LAST

~

On the night of a new moon, write your wish on a bay leaf. Take the bay leaf outside and look at the moon, then kiss the leaf three times and sleep with it under your pillow.

FOR BETTER SELF-ESTEEM

~

Hold a hand mirror and light a candle. Look into the mirror and study your face. Think about your best qualities, inside and out. Say the following chant:

Mirror of mystery, beauty, and light,
Bring my true spirit into sight!
May I become better inside and out!
I accept my power, without a doubt!

Study yourself in the mirror once more. Focus only on your good qualities and tell yourself how beautiful you are.

TO END A RELATIONSHIP

~

To sever the ties that bind you to another, visualize a white cord tied first to your waist and then to his or hers. Say to yourself:

You broke your promise.
And now it is done.
Our bond is severed, no joy, no fun.
I cut the cord that held on tight,
Now I am free to do what is right.

Visualize cutting the cord between you. You are not bound to him or her in this life and can move forward with an open heart.

TO RELEASE SADNESS

~

Make yourself a cup of chamomile tea and breathe in the aroma. Get comfortable and relax.

As you relax and breathe in, imagine the light of happiness flowing into you. As you breathe out, imagine the darkness of depression leaving. Try to remember the times you were the happiest in your life and visualize that energy of joy and contentment flowing through you.

TO FIND FREEDOM FROM WORRY

~

Clean out a jar with a tight-fitting lid. Write the problem on a slip of paper. Place it in the jar while reciting the following spell:

I hold my worry in a jar,
The problem will my mind not mar.
If I can keep it out of my head,
I'll bury my worry,
As if it were dead.

When the problem is resolved, remove the slip of paper and bury it.

TO GET OVER ANGER

~

Write the following on a piece of paper three times:

Let anger and despair depart.
I allow a healing in my heart.
Bring love and peace instead to me.
So I can be who I am supposed to be.

Fold the paper and place it into a heat-resistant dish. Carefully light it with a match and allow it to burn down into ash.

Feel the pain of the anger in the relationship burning away while the flames of anger die down to embers, then ash. When cool enough to handle, bury the ashes deep in the earth.

FOR OPENING YOUR HEART
TO A NEW LOVE

~

Bathe in water scented with perfume or rose oil. Allow the stresses of the day to float away and, when you are done, to escape down the drain. Apply lotion all over your body, increasing circulation. Dress in red. Wear jewelry with red stones. Carve the nature of your desire for a new love, in your own words, on a red candle with a needle. Speak your wish aloud and feel your desire for a new love, calling upon the deity of your choice as you watch the candle flame. Visualize a red color glowing vividly all around your body. Feel your heart open. Blow out the candle.

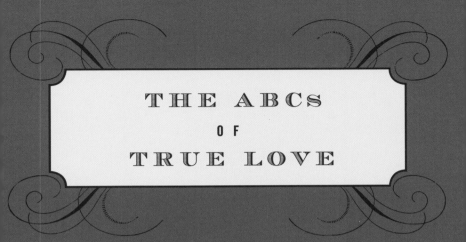

THE ABCs
OF
TRUE LOVE

~ A ~

APPRECIATE all the good things in life. Show your love. Show you care. Passion and compassion are what make you attractive. If you would enjoy the passion of love, you must act first with passion. Men are willing to go through a lot to earn the appreciation of their true love, and women, as the keepers of the sacred flame of life, desire to be given the respect they deserve. If you demonstrate your mutual appreciation, true love will deepen and last a very long time.

~ B ~

BE PLAYFUL and have fun. Encourage a sense of adventure. Try to maintain a positive, open attitude even when things don't appear to be going the way you want. Much of the art of living is dealing with the unexpected. See with the eyes of a child. Enjoy yourself and celebrate.

~ C ~

CULTIVATE contentment in all circumstances. Self-doubt is the most daunting of obstacles that inhibit us on our quest for enlightenment. We can know true contentment when we embrace the present and stop struggling to escape insecurity, pain, and doubt.

~ D ~

DUALITY is the central organizing principle of our reality. We cannot know what light is unless we know darkness. We cannot know the meaning of sweet without knowing the meaning of sour. It follows that we cannot know what we like without also experiencing that which we do not like.

~ E ~

EXPRESS yourself creatively. You need to be appreciated for who you really are. Speak and let others know. Communication begins with an effort to make yourself clearly understood. It is easy to let fear and preconceived notions stand in the way of true communication. Taking an interest in how others express themselves (known as listening!) leads to sharing, and sharing leads to caring. Creative self-expression is true spirituality.

~ F ~

FORGIVENESS is an antidote to pain. All too often the tendency is not to try to solve the problem but to fix the blame. It is not a weakness but the greatest strength to forgive. Especially, forgive yourself. Accept your human frailty as a natural part of your being and your mistakes as signs of your efforts to grow.

~ G ~

GROWTH comes through self-examination and self-awareness. Know thyself. In our case, it was commitment to our mutual goal of personal development that has allowed us to learn and help each other grow. We may not know the meaning of life, but we have come to know the meaning of our life.

~ H ~

HAVING A SENSE OF HUMOR is a tremendous asset when it comes to relationships. It is one of the most valuable and attractive features a person can have. If you keep looking for the humor in your situation, not only will you find it, but also it can get you through practically any difficult time. It helps you keep going forward, even in the face of defeat.

~ I ~

INTUITION is your inner vision—let it guide you. Become aware, pay attention, listen—develop a psychic sense of your and your partner's true feelings. Validate each other's intuition. By observing our reactions to the messages offered to us by our intuition, we come to understand our desires, our goals, and others' motivations better. We come to see what blocks us, what releases us from our false selves, and what helps us meet the challenge of our personal vision and myth.

~ J ~

JUDGMENT has its time and place. Let it help you be relentless in your pursuit of truth and the deeper implications of whatever situation you are in. Remember, criticism must be constructive, not a smokescreen for hurtful words and deeds. Judge the truth and judge the lies.

~ K ~

KNOW you have the power to defeat negative thinking and behavior. Learn to understand and cope with your greatest enemy, your own fear. We have learned that living a successful life of quality and meaning does not mean you won't react to fear, uncertainty, or rejection. What is important is how quickly you recover your equilibrium and get on with the business of living.

~ L ~

LOVE makes a sacred space in our lives where true growth and healing can happen. When we love and are loved, we have someone we can trust to advise us, someone who has our best interests at heart. When you love someone, you want to be with him or her as much as possible because committed happiness makes life seem very short, indeed.

~ M ~

MAKE MAGIC, pray, consult the wise. Real magic is when you concentrate on what you love, not what you hate. Believe there are unseen forces that protect, connect, and sustain us. When we see the hidden connections, the world becomes charged with symbolic meanings. Magic rituals and prayers help us remember our connection to unlimited energies that nurture and beckon us to reach our full potential, and we will do the work necessary to keep that connection clear and unbroken. Prayer is a form of magic in which we seek to ally ourselves with the divine.

~ N ~

NATURE teaches us about life's cycles. The entire world is alive with messages and it speaks to us if we will only listen. Nature reminds us of the abundant beauty present in everyday life. Make a time and space in your day, when and where you won't be disturbed, to listen to all that is good in your life "speak." The goal is to be so in harmony with life's purpose that we instinctively know which paths to follow from the many that present themselves each day.

~ O ~

OBSERVE how your habitual thoughts affect your life. It is the nature of habits to rule us unless we first become aware that they are habits, examine the events that gave rise to them, and pay attention to how they actively influence us. The only way to eliminate a habit is through patient awareness and the belief that your life will change for the better if you stop acting or thinking in the old, habitual way.

~ P ~

PEACE begins when expectations end. There is a goodness in things as they are—accept the greater purpose behind frustrating circumstances. The present moment is your point of power. The secret of contentment can't be gained from achievements in the world but only from finding inner peace.

~ Q ~

QUEST FOR TRUTH. When you have taken the time and done the work of establishing initial truthfulness and trust, you will find it frees up an incredible amount of energy that can be used to accomplish many important things. Remember, you cannot be truthful with another person unless you are first truthful with yourself.

~ R ~

RESPECT yourself and show that same respect for others. If you find it difficult to respect yourself, be aware that the most respectable people also have feelings of self-doubt. Self-doubt may never leave, but those who come to respect themselves learn to accept themselves as they are. Root out prejudiced ideas in yourself and be aware of them in others. Equal partners make successful relationships. There is no other way.

~ S ~

SOUL MATES work on their relationships by working on themselves. You know you have found your soul mate when you enjoy just watching your partner live and when you desire to make your partnership work and to be there for each other in every way.

~ T ~

TRUST the process. Have faith that there is a divine plan. Worry only creates stress and accomplishes nothing. If you realize most difficulties you encounter are for the best in the long run, you manifest the positive attitude that can bring wonderful relationships to you. All you have to do is follow your heart, take small steps forward on your path, and trust. Let the future wait and take care of itself. Take time to be in the moment and experience life with a gentle purity.

~ U ~

UNCONDITIONAL LOVE helps you be more understanding. Your lover is your best friend—you must be there for each other in every way. You must feel you can trust one another completely and can turn to each other for support and gentle guidance when one of you feels weak. Remember, a maternal nature exists in us all.

~ V ~

VISUALIZE your wishes in your mind's eye. Become aware of the tone and subject matter of your moment-to-moment inner dialogue. Visualize what it is you want with all your heart. See it with your inner sight and feel it as if you were really there experiencing it with all your senses. Practice visualization every day. Our dreams help us create our material reality as surely as our material reality helps us create our dreams.

~ W ~

WORKING TOWARD GOALS together is the essence of a living, breathing partnership. Give support as needed. Concentrate and focus your energy on positive goals: health, fitness, creativity, spiritual growth. When you share love, you can enjoy knowing you are helping your partner live to the fullest. This is the secret of true joy and happiness in a committed relationship. Our relationship is as successful as it is because we have both decided it is the most important thing in our lives.

~ X ~

XOX. KISSES AND HUGS are very important. Physical touch is the healing catalyst that allows your souls to connect and become one. Sex is one of the highest forms of expression when combined with true love. It is heightened and enlightened by mutual intimacy, trust, and joyful commitment. Without love, sex becomes just another way to avoid feeling empty. Real love is exciting because the two of you care so much about each other and want to show it in every way.

~ Y ~

YOU CAN CHANGE only yourself. You cannot change anyone else. You can, however, make sure you get involved with a person who desires change for the better. Devoting time to study or self-improvement will always enable you to improve your situation. The desire to grow is one of our most basic needs.

~ Z ~

Z-Z-Z. GET ENOUGH REST and take care of your stress. Listen to your dreams. Practice calm. Slow down your breathing. Manage your time. Know your stress triggers. Laugh as much as possible. Get massages. Explore healing practices designed to cure problems on physical, mental, and spiritual levels. You must heal yourself before you can help others heal.

ABOUT THE AUTHORS

Internationally known self-help author Monte Farber's inspiring guidance and empathic insights impact everyone he encounters. Amy Zerner's exquisite, one-of-a-kind, spiritual couture creations and collaged fabric paintings exude her profound intuition and deep connection with archetypal stories and healing energies. For nearly thirty years they've combined their deep love for one another with the work of inner-exploration and self-discovery to build The Enchanted World of Amy Zerner and Monte Farber: books, card decks, and oracles that have helped millions answer questions, find deeper meaning, and follow their own spiritual paths.

Together they've made their love for one another a work of art and their art the work of their lives. Their best-selling titles include: *The Chakra Meditation Kit*, *The Enchanted Tarot*, *The Instant Tarot Reader*, *The Psychic Circle*, *Karma Cards*, *The Pathfinder Psychic Talking Board*, *The Oracle of the Goddess*, *The Truth Fairy*, *The Healing Deck*, *The Zerner/Farber Tarot Deck*, *The Breathe Easy Deck*, *The Animal Powers Meditation Kit*, and *Gifts of the Goddess Affirmation Cards*.

FOR FURTHER INFORMATION PLEASE WRITE TO:
The Enchanted World of Amy Zerner and Monte Farber
Attn: *True Love Tarot*
Post Office Box 2299
East Hampton, NY 11937 USA
OR
E-mail: info@TheEnchantedWorld.com

Please visit Amy and Monte's amazing Web site, www.TheEnchantedWorld.com, where you can not only learn more about them and their work, but you can get free tarot, astrology, and alchemy readings, your daily affirmations, eCards of Amy's gorgeous art, and a lot more! Their Enchanted World Web site is a no-pressure, ad-free, enchanted oasis of peace, beauty, and wisdom that you and those you care about will enjoy and want to share. There's nothing like it on the World Wide Web.